FAREWELL TO MANZANAR

NOTES

including
- *Life and Background of the Authors*
- *Introduction to the Novel*
- *Historical Perspective*
- *A Brief Synopsis*
- *List of Characters*
- *Chronology*
- *Maps*
- *Genealogy Chart*
- *Critical Commentaries*
- *Critical Essays*
- *Character Analyses*
- *Review Questions and Essay Topics*
- *Selected Bibliography*

DISCARDE

by
Mei Li Robinson, M.A.
University of North Carolina at Greensboro

D1510928

Cliffs®Notes
INCORPORATED
LINCOLN, NEBRASKA 68501

OIL CITY LIBRARY
2 CENTRAL AVENUE
OIL CITY, PA. 16301

Editor

Gary Carey, M.A.
University of Colorado

Consulting Editor

James L. Roberts, Ph.D.
Department of English
University of Nebraska

The author and editor thank Jeanne and James Houston for supplying
research materials, commentary, and support of these Notes.

ISBN 0-8220-0463-1
© Copyright 1993
by
Cliffs Notes, Inc.
All Rights Reserved
Printed in U.S.A.

1994 Printing

The Cliffs Notes logo, the names "Cliffs" and "Cliffs Notes," and
the black and yellow diagonal-stripe cover design are all registered
trademarks belonging to Cliffs Notes, Inc., and may not be used in
whole or in part without written permission.

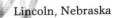

Cliffs Notes, Inc.   Lincoln, Nebraska

CONTENTS

Centerfold: *Farewell to Manzanar* Genealogy

FAREWELL TO MANZANAR

Notes

LIFE AND BACKGROUND OF THE AUTHORS

Introduction. In a straightforward, nonfiction **memoir,** Jeanne Wakatsuki Houston and her husband, James D. Houston, recount the Wakatsuki family's internment at Manzanar War Relocation Center, one of ten concentration camps devised by President Franklin Roosevelt's Executive Order 9066 following the Japanese surprise bombing of Pearl Harbor on December 7, 1941. To some readers, the book is an introduction to a thorny era in their country's history, a time of deprivation of rights without due process for 120,000 Japanese Americans. Jeanne's reliving of intimate, painful details provides what no historical account can—a view of life for 30,000 Asian Americans in a stark, concentration-camp atmosphere on the rim of California's Mojave Desert. The factual narrative follows her through three decades of silent denial to adulthood, when she is, at last, able to reveal the misery, the degradation of her family and race, and exorcise Manzanar with an act of public enlightenment.

Jeanne's Early Years. For Jeanne Toyo Wakatsuki, childhood security flowed naturally from the loving, accepting kin who made up her household. Born in Inglewood, California, on September 26, 1934, to native Japanese parents, Ko and Riku Sugai Wakatsuki, Jeanne, the youngest of four boys and six girls, moved with her family to Ocean Park in 1936. In an interview, she recalled the pier as a magical place, "my nursery school, the amusement attendants my sitters." She grew up admiring the strutting self-confidence of her father, a farmer and commercial fisherman, and her pragmatic, low-key mother, who worked in a Long Beach fish cannery. Prophetic of Jeanne's individualism, the Wakatsukis had met in Spokane, Washington, eloped, and married for love, defying an arranged engagement between Riku and a farmer.

Jeanne's female role models, evolved from two previous generations, helped develop a sense of self, a concept deeply rooted in the Japanese separation of male and female roles. Her maternal grandmother, although restricted by blindness and speaking no English, served as a link with Japan, as demonstrated by old country treasures she handled delicately—the lacquered tables and fragile blue and white porcelain tea service, reminiscent of a genteel culture incompatible with her new home in the United States. Jeanne's mother understood and accepted her place in a patriarchal marriage. With less time to devote to the niceties of serving tea than her aged mother enjoyed, she resigned herself to the thankless jobs of scrubbing floors, washing clothes, cooking, waiting on Ko, and tending her ten children. When Jeanne expressed terror that her *Oka-San* might drop dead from overwork, Riku soothed, "I'm not a washerwoman. This is just a chore, something I must do because I'm a woman, but foremost, I'm your mother."

Jeanne was seven years old when the bombing of Pearl Harbor plunged the U.S. into World War II. The Wakatsukis, their lives interrupted during a post-Depression upsurge in family finances, were among the first to be questioned and detained. FBI agents confronted Ko with photos of barrels of fish bait and accused him of supplying oil to enemy submarines. Although the charge was unfounded in a court of law, he spent nine months apart from his clan in a Bismarck, North Dakota, prison. During his imprisonment, in April 1942 his wife and son Woody assumed responsibility for resettling the family in Block 16 of Manzanar, an austere, barbed-wire enclosed, mile-square internment camp near Lone Pine, California, 4,000 feet above sea level in the shadow of Mount Whitney.

From her early memories of Mama, Papa, Woody, brother Kiyo, sister May, sister-in-law Chizu, and others came the book *Farewell to Manzanar* (1973), a retelling of Jeanne's girlhood traumas and dreams in the milieu of an artificial Japanese-American city, the largest metropolis (10,000 Japanese Americans) between Reno and Los Angeles. She recalls the experience as a yellow blur of "stinging whirlwinds and fierce dust storms that pricked the skin like needles and coated everything, including our lips and eyelashes, with thick ochre powder."

Amid rows of dreary barracks, functional mess halls and latrines, and intimidating gatehouses and fences, she and her peers lived out a semblance of normality, singing in the glee club, acting in school plays, enjoying the taste of her first snowflake, and wondering how the inflamed white populace would accept them when Japanese Americans were finally released from custody. She recalled later a major source of comfort: she discovered an abandoned box of books in a firebreak and escaped camp misery through Hans Christian Andersen's *Fairy Tales*, Nancy Drew mysteries, James Fenimore Cooper's Leatherstocking series, and Emily Brontë's *Wuthering Heights*.

In September 1942, Ko, an embittered ex-con, was transferred to Manzanar from a North Dakota prison. His reclusive habits and escapism through home-distilled rice wine ignited explosive domestic violence—threats, shoving, and screaming. Jeanne and her youngest brother hid as far under the covers as possible, but the limited quarters afforded no privacy or respite from daily turmoil. To distance herself from home, Jeanne stayed outdoors, twirled her baton, and studied traditional Japanese dancing. For a time, she flirted with Catholicism by losing herself in the melodrama of saints' and martyrs' lives and the dogma of catechism. Ko's refusal to allow her to be converted and baptized, however, narrowed her outlets to school and dance.

The close-knit Wakatsukis began breaking up as older siblings moved to job opportunities on nearby farms and through military service. In November 1944, Woody entered active service and was shipped to Germany. That winter, occupancy at Manzanar dropped to twenty percent. Ko, fearful of West Coast anti-Japanese hysteria, resisted departure until October 1945, when his name came up for forced expulsion. His crazy, drunken departure in a new car forms the ebullient conclusion to Jeanne's memoir.

Back to Normal Life. In Cabrillo Homes, a cheerless multicultural housing project in Long Beach, Jeanne maintained her new, all-American attitude, twirling her baton, singing the country-western tunes of Roy Acuff and Red Foley, and learning Spanish tunes as well. She coped with overt racism in the form of taunts, exclusion from Girl Scouts, and outright ignorance of locals who considered her a foreigner. To compensate for a free-floating belief that she somehow deserved exclusion, she excelled at school, discovered a knack for writing while working as editor of the school paper, the *Chatterbox*, and achieved two youthful goals: she became a majorette and a beauty queen. In *Beyond Manzanar*, Jeanne admits that during the teen period of assimilative behavior, she was "trying to be as American as Doris Day."

Ko disapproved of Jeanne's bold, sweater-girl look and rebuked her for immodestly strutting, a quality she no doubt acquired from him. Although he resisted the Americanization of his youngest child, Jeanne's mother accepted the fact that Jeanne was behaving normally, including falling in love with a soft-spoken neighbor boy from North Carolina, who taught her to kiss, then parted without leaving a forwarding address. In 1952, the Wakatsukis themselves moved from Cabrillo Homes to a rural, more amenable setting in San Jose, where Ko grew strawberries for Driscoll, Inc.

Jeanne, the Wakatsukis' iconoclast, brought two firsts to the family—a college diploma and the first non-Asian dates. She was attracted to Caucasian males, yet longed to meet a combination of American sensitivity and Japanese potency—in her words, "I wanted a blond Samurai." In her sophomore year, she contemplated a career in journalism, but faced the fact that writing jobs were usually reserved for male reporters. Like other Asians, she opted for an "invisible field" and pursued a sociology degree from the University of San Jose, enrolled in San Francisco State, attended the Sorbonne in Paris, and worked from 1955 to 1957 as a social worker at a juvenile detention hall and probation officer in San Mateo, California.

Jeanne and James. While living in San Jose, Jeanne met teacher James D. Houston. Born November 10, 1933, in San Francisco, the son of Texas blacksmith and sharecropper Albert Dudley Houston (a distant kin of Texas hero Sam Houston) and Alice Loretta Wilson Houston, James grew up in a fundamentalist southern milieu. He graduated from Lowell High School in San Francisco, earned degrees from San Jose State College and Stanford University, and achieved the rank of lieutenant in the U.S. Air Force.

James courted Jeanne long distance from Hawaii with a valentine and proposal inscribed on a ti leaf, which withered to brown by the time it traversed the ocean in a mail pouch. She responded by flying to Hawaii to marry her Caucasian sweetheart. The flower-decked couple had a romantic barefoot wedding at sunset on Waikiki Beach.

Jeanne lived a Jekyll-and-Hyde existence—sometimes being engagingly subservient like her mother; at other times, being independent like American wives. That fall, James was transferred to an ROTC post in England and Jeanne got her first taste of bone-chilling English winters, living in a ten-room townhouse reminiscent of scenes from Dickens. In 1962, the year after the birth of daughter Corinne, nicknamed Cori, the family was back in the U.S., where James taught English at Cabrillo College in Aptos, California.

In 1967, James published *Gig*, earning the Joseph Henry Jackson award from the San Francisco Foundation, and accepted the Wallace Stegner creative writing fellowship at Stanford; that same year, Jeanne gave birth to twins, Joshua and Gabrielle. Following the publication of his novel *Between Battles*, James advanced to the University of California in 1969.

Manzanar, repressed in Jeanne's memory, resurfaced in 1971 when one of her nephews, her oldest sister Eleanor's son Gary Nishikawa, asked her to share her memories, since other clan members hedged on details. Gary had been born in Manzanar, and his insistence on full disclosure brought Jeanne to the brink of hysteria. Her subsequent attempts to compose a memoir forced a confession of her longing to relieve traumatic childhood insecurity through writing. James, who had known her for twenty years, had no idea of her secret shame. He proposed that she write "a story everyone in America should read."

The next year, while James enjoyed a University of California faculty research grant, the Houston family traveled to Manzanar, where Jeanne confronted the persistent memories that plagued her subconscious. As her children frolicked on the desert, she strolled through decaying relics of the abandoned windswept internment camp. In an interview with the *Los Angeles Times,* she admitted feeling "sullied, like when you are a rape victim. . . . You feel you must have *done* something. You feel you are a part of the act." The return to Manzanar prompted a catharsis as she extracted herself from internment and viewed it objectively as a moment in history.

From Jeanne's confrontation of this undeserved humiliation grew *Farewell to Manzanar,* a husband-and-wife collaboration recreating Jeanne's childhood memories and adult acceptance of one of democracy's most blatant injustices. The Houstons' working method blended Jeanne's tape recorded dialogue with library research, three field excursions to Manzanar, and interviews with family and other internees. The outcome, more than a publishable manuscript, brought Jeanne a combination of becalmed spirit and will to write. She described her emergent self this way: "I realized I could no longer hide in the country of my husband's shadow."

Dual Careers. Jeanne Houston's self-directed psychotherapy initiated a full career. She and James joined with producer-director John Korty to script the TV screenplay "Farewell to Manzanar" for Universal and MCA-TV. The film version premiered as the NBC "Thursday Night at the Movies" feature on March 11, 1976, the year that James earned a National Endowment for the Arts creative writing grant. Well received for its historical accuracy, the film featured the Houston twins, actor Lou Frizell in one of the few Caucasian speaking parts, and Japanese-American employees and internees of Tule Lake, Heart Mountain, Minidoka, and Topaz internment camps. Most of the Asian-American cast, including Jimmy Nakamura, Akemi Kikumura, Nobu McCarthy as Mama, and Yuki Shimoda as Ko Wakatsuki, brought to their jobs a sincere interest in an historical event which impinged on their race. Shimoda remarked, "I felt that the role of Ko was the role I have been preparing for all these years. . . . The feeling on the set is like no other picture I have worked in."

Designer Robert Kinoshita recreated Manzanar 400 miles northwest of its location at Tule Lake, California, at the only extant internment facility, where he used tarpaper and lath over pine planking to emulate temporary, substandard quarters. In the scene in which Ko enters Manzanar, Nobu McCarthy, unable to separate herself from the character she portrayed, grasped Shimoda and sobbed into his chest. He comforted her with an understanding embrace. Jeanne was so moved by the scene that she wept for "the pride of my father—the humiliation, the stubbornness, the shattered dignity."

The movie won a Humanitas Prize, a Christopher Award, and an Emmy nomination for best dramatic script adapted from another medium. Judith Crist, critic for *TV Guide*, lauded the movie as a "deeply moving examination of family relations under stress and of the scars that remain." *Time's* Richard Schickel, in his March 15, 1976, review described the movie as "modest and touching and refreshingly free of melodrama." More philosophical was *Newsweek's* comment that same week, "The cruelties that men visit on one another can, at least in retrospect, help them to perceive their common humanity."

The Houston duo continued their probe of multicultural themes with back-to-back books, *Beyond Manzanar and Other Views of Asian-American Womanhood* and *One Can Think About Life After the Fish Is in the Canoe and Other Coastal Stories* (1985), and *Barrio*, an eight-part miniseries for NBC. On their own, the Houstons function as solo writers and lecturers. Jeanne fills her days with writing articles for *Mother Jones, California, West, California Living, Reader's Digest*, and the *New England Review* and by speaking at West Coast, Hawaiian, and Asian campuses. James has produced a composition text, biography, essays, novels, and stories in *Playboy, Michigan Quarterly Review, Yardbird Reader, Unknown California, Bennington Review, Honolulu, Manoa, Rolling Stone*, and *Mother Jones*, as well as articles for the *New York Times* and *Los Angeles Times*. His best-received nonfiction, *Californians: Searching for the Golden State* (1982), earned a Before Columbus Foundation American Book Award.

Jeanne's contribution to the reclamation of the Asian-American past has netted her recognition from the National Women's Political Caucus. In 1984, after meriting Warner Communications' Wonder Woman award for "the pursuit of truth and positive social change," she and James, on a tour of Japan, the Philippines, Korea, Malaysia, and Indonesia, visited refugee camps. More recent honors include the East-West Center award from the 1989 Hawaii International Film Festival and a U.S.-Japan Cultural Exchange fellowship in 1991, during which the Houstons spent six months in Japan. Although close enough to visit Hiroshima, Jeanne chose not to view the place where members of the Wakatsuki family were incinerated by an atomic bomb.

Actively pursuing their trade, Jeanne and James Houston, their children grown, still live in their Victorian house in Santa Cruz and work out of separate office spaces. In her third-floor studio, Jeanne is at work on a new novel. An upbeat, positive woman, petite and graceful next to Jim's tall, lanky good looks, Jeanne, despite her family's sufferings, rejects a hostile, anti-American stance in favor of a humanistic embrace of democracy. Like Jim, she defines herself as a "philosophic Buddhist," attuned to peace, harmony, and nonviolence.

In a recent interview, she acknowledged that it took years for her to forgive her father for his pomposity and the violent episodes which allowed him to submerge his shame in alcohol and inappropriate outbursts. Fortunately for the family, he quit drinking after physical symptoms indicated that he was shortening his life. He died in 1957. Jeanne, along with her surviving six siblings, treasures the positive images of Ko Wakatsuki, particularly his faith in the American dream. In her lectures, she emphasizes "how far, as a country, we have come in our understanding and practice of human rights. My discussion neither lays guilt nor attacks. In the final analysis, it is an affirmation of what America really is."

INTRODUCTION TO THE NOVEL

In the tradition of eyewitness accounts, *Farewell to Manzanar* convinces readers through a sincere, **objective** recounting of events in the girlhood of Jeanne Wakatsuki. As historically correct as Samuel Pepys' recollections of the London fire and the restoration of Charles II to the throne of England, as passionately devoted to righting injustice as Elie Wiesel's *Night*, as tenderly innocent and family centered as *The Diary of Anne Frank*, the Houstons' book earns critical acclaim for **verisimilitude**. Notable critics have placed the book in its own niche; a *Los Angeles Times* reporter praised Jeanne for serving as a "voice for a heretofore silent segment of society." Others have similar praise.

Writer-critic Wallace Stegner typifies the work as "a wonderful, human, feeling book . . . touching, funny, affectionate, sad, eager, and forgiving. And full of understanding . . . [it] manages to become a scale model of all our lives."

In a vivid personal response for *The Nation* (November 9, 1974), Dorothy Bryant makes a significant delineation between the book and other autobiographical journeys: "The Houstons are not simply trying to communicate facts as Jeanne knew them, but were themselves on a search to touch the truth of her experience, to examine it, and to understand it wholly. The great strength of the book is the sense it gives the reader of being allowed to accompany Jeanne on this most personal and intimate journey."

Katherine Anderson of *Library Journal* (January 15, 1974) lauds the way in which Jeanne candidly divulges "the psychological impact of being Japanese in California during World War II," yet avoids self-pity and bitterness.

A terse, unsigned review in the *New York Times Book Review* (November 5, 1973) notes the devastating effects of Jeanne's "spiritual death" under tense camp conditions. The critique concludes: "Although there are brief recreations of some of the internal ferment at the camp, the deeper political and social implications of Manzanar are largely ignored . . . [this] book [however] provides an often vivid, **impressionistic** picture of how the forced isolation affected the internees. All in all, a dramatic, telling account of one of the most reprehensible events in the history of America's treatment of its minorities."

An unsigned review in the *New Yorker* (January 13, 1974) concurs that "a particularly ignominious chapter in our history is recounted with chilling simplicity by an internee," particularly in its detailed dissection of Ko, who "was too old to bend with the humiliations of the camp. . . . His story is at the heart of this book, and his daughter tells it with great dignity."

Equally impressed by the unenhanced memoir is Helen Rabinowitz in her review for *Saturday Review* (November 6, 1973): "Mrs. Houston and her husband have recorded a tale of many complexities in a straightforward manner, a tale remarkably lacking in either self-pity or solemnity. It is the record of one woman's maturation during a unique historical moment."

Michael Rogers, reviewing for *Rolling Stone* (December 6, 1973), concludes that the book "avoids sentimentality, however, by remaining true to its intention: to illuminate at once the experience of a people, of a family, and of an individual."

In a more scholarly appraisal, Anthony Friedson delineates the Houstons' reflective book on three levels: first, an overview of war hysteria; second, an episode in American assimilation; third, a **coming-of-age narrative** focusing on Jeanne's growing-up years. Produced to fill a void, the book, intended as **polemic,** or aggressive statement of opinion, on a controversial issue, authenticates a significant page in America's history, a confrontation with the bedrock issues of freedoms as old as the Magna Carta and guaranteed in the Constitution. Because no previous work dealt so intimately with the denial of freedoms to Asian Americans, the Houstons' research lays the groundwork for more scholarship and narrative as a means to greater understanding of racism.

Not only does the work illuminate the political maneuverings which cost 120,000 innocent people over three years of unconstitutional incarceration, it also details the social mechanisms by which people cope with arbitrary uprooting, loss, privation, and national embarrassment. Told in readable, accessible form, the book skirts a more academic approach by relying on **first-person narration** from a child's perspective. Chronologically, the work concludes, not with the closing of the internment camp, but with the marriage of Jeanne to a Caucasian. In a healing, unifying return to Manzanar, the speaker creates a conciliatory **tone**, a method of ridding herself of lingering regrets and bitterness and of assisting her race and her nation to reflect on an episode as shattering and dismaying as the massacre at Wounded Knee, the Salem witch trials, Nat Turner's rebellion, John Brown's hanging, the Battle of the Little Big Horn, the Watts, Attica Prison, and Los Angeles riots, the exploitation of coolie labor to build the transcontinental railroad, or the My Lai massacre.

HISTORICAL PERSPECTIVE

The War Years. The bombing of Pearl Harbor, Hawaii, in an early morning surprise attack did irreparable harm to ostensibly friendly Japanese-American relations, which had been proceeding on a basis of candor and mutual respect. At 6 A.M. on Sunday, December 7, 1941, Vice Admiral Chuichi Nagumo led six carriers, two battleships, three cruisers, and a fleet of destroyers and tanks from the Kuril Islands toward Pearl Harbor, a major American naval headquarters on the southern coast of Oahu in the territory of Hawaii. By 7:50 A.M., the first wave of Japanese bombers had struck battleships and airfields. At 10:00 A.M., a second wave had completed its mission and was jubilantly returning to base. Of the eighteen U.S. ships hit, the *Arizona, West Virginia, California,* and *Nevada* sustained the most damage. Over 200 planes were crippled or wrecked, 2,400 people died, 1,300 were wounded, and more than 1,000 were missing. With enemy losses of only 29 planes, 5 submarines, and 100 soldiers, the Japanese had reason to cheer about their advantageous strike. They had seriously crippled naval preparedness by blocking the harbor so that U.S. ships could not retaliate and overtake the Japanese fleet.

The day after the raid, President Franklin Roosevelt read to Congress his **proclamation** that December 7, 1941, was "a date which will live in infamy." Smarting under critical attack that he had left Pearl Harbor unprotected in order to provoke an attack, Roosevelt overrode Secretary of State Cordell Hull's role and assumed total command of the war effort. Following Roosevelt's impassioned declaration of war against Japan, a Caucasian backlash in racially mixed communities along the western U.S. coastline provoked incidents of name-calling, minor scuffles and rock-throwing, graffiti, hate crimes, boycotting of Asian-owned businesses, and signs saying "Japs, don't let the sun set on you here," "Hiring whites only," and "Buy bonds. Bye-bye Japs."

On February 19, 1942, the issuance of Executive Order 9066 followed the FBI's arrest of more than 700 Japanese-American males, partly in retribution for the Pearl Harbor attack. The American Civil Liberties Union, outraged at Roosevelt's racism, later labeled the detention "the greatest deprivation of civil liberties by government in this country since slavery." In their recent interview for *Mother Jones*, the Houstons listed reasons for the U.S. government's unprecedented suspension of citizens' rights:

- anti-Asian agitation on the U.S. West Coast,

- reaction to economic competition between Caucasians and Japanese Americans, and

- wartime hysteria, which threatened Asians with outbreaks of violence.

Californians, fearing collusion which might lead to a landing of enemy forces or the sabotage of dams or power plants, conspired to violate Japanese-American freedoms. Mayors, governors, legislators, and the American Legion joined with the media to force removal of Japanese Americans, although no evidence of either espionage or sabotage was ever found.

Eventually, more than 3,000 Japanese-American men were imprisoned—not interned, but imprisoned—even though they remained overwhelmingly pro-American. Many of these were **Issei** [ee' say], like Ko Wakatsuki—native-born Japanese immigrants who had survived the Depression and were just beginning to realize dreams of financial prosperity when internment snatched away the fruits of their labors. The only area in which this pattern did not prevail was Hawaii, where the population depended too heavily on Japanese labor to confine or idle valuable workers.

Internment. On March 24, 1942, the first load of civilian evacuees, carrying small amounts of personal belongings, were transported to camps. Two-thirds of the internees were **Nisei** [nee' say], American citizens born to Japanese immigrant parents, whose rights were spelled out in the U.S. Constitution as it is for citizens of all races. The press sugarcoated the primitive camps as having "all the comforts of home" and reminded the evacuees that they entered camps "not as prisoners but free to work." Analysts believe that white entrepreneurs, envious of the Japanese-American success in farming, fishing, and manufacturing, pressed for this militaristic incarceration of their competitors and profited by their absence. Whatever the thinking of authorities, the government's attitude was made obvious by one overriding fact—camp guns were aimed inward *at* internees rather than outward at potential attackers.

Internment wrenched apart Asian communities and herded people from farms, ranches, and homes into ten hastily constructed internment camps in Arizona, Arkansas, Colorado, Utah, Wyoming, Idaho, and California. Left behind were homes and cars, businesses and personal belongings, most of which were never recovered from last-minute storage, bank repossession, or abandonment. Ahead lay barbed wire compounds with guardhouses constructed at frequent intervals and cramped accommodations for eight to sixteen thousand detainees. Resembling army bases with barracks arranged in blocks, the ten camps began as an army project, but were eventually placed under the War Relocation Authority.

The camps offered no play areas for children, who often scrounged seashells at Manzanar from a valley which was once an ocean. Although inmates lacked autonomy, life was made bearable at the dust-drenched Manzanar camp by a spirit of unity, which encouraged people to go on with learning, singing, gardening, exercise, visiting, and friendships. The Manzanar High School yearbooks record plays, chorus and orchestra performances, and musicals. Camp records list births as well as deaths.

The Rebels. Out of 120,000, only three Japanese-Americans refused to be badgered or to surrender their rights—Quaker pacifist

Gordon Kiyoshi Hirabayashi, a former Eagle Scout and honor student; Minoru Yasui, a Portland, Oregon, lawyer; and Fred Korematsu, a welder in the San Leandro, California, shipyards. The most adamant, Hirabayashi, remained true to his ideal that rights belong to *all* Americans, regardless of race or national heritage. Acting on the advice of a Quaker lawyer, Hirabayashi disobeyed curfews for Asians, then turned himself over to the FBI for refusing internment and breaking curfew. Hirabayashi drew a jail term. Other Japanese Americans ostracized him for rebelling.

On October 20, 1942, Hirabayashi went to trial, where the judge refused him due process on the issue of violation of civil rights and found him guilty of breaking the law. Hirabayashi, assured that an appeal to the Supreme Court would end mass internment, opted to go to prison. On June 21, 1943, he discovered that his supposition was faulty—the Supreme Court upheld internment as a necessary emergency measure in the interest of national security. Only Justice Frank Murphy dissented from the majority opinion by comparing internment to the Nazi oppression of Jews.

Justice Murphy's most famous civil rights stand came in 1944 with *Korematsu v. United States*, a case in which he labeled as racist the wartime internment of Japanese Americans. However, his support for Constitutional rights did not spare Hirabayashi from the injustice of internment, compounded by having to pay his own way to Camp Tule. It was only after Roosevelt's third election that pressure to release Japanese Americans brought about a rescinding of Executive Order 9066 and the release of internees who passed the loyalty tests.

The Japanese-American Warrior. While less flexible civilian Issei fought internal battles over family rights and loyalty oaths, 1,000 Nisei males signed up for military service. Young and inexperienced, Japanese-American soldiers, particularly those fluent in Japanese, proved vital to the war effort and earned more medals than any other unit. Although not advanced to ranks higher than sergeant, they served as teachers to intelligence officers and prepared plans so that a smooth occupation of Japan might end the war with a negligible loss of life to both the American military and civilian Japanese. The most valued of the Nisei were the **Kibei** [kee' bay], Japanese Americans who had trained in Japan and who knew the terrain, language, and customs well enough to pass for natives.

The Kibei deciphered Japanese code and eavesdropped on Japanese radio transmissions. They translated intercepted documents, which detailed troop and convoy movements, ship locations, reinforcement strength, and direction of supply lines. Like Tokyo Rose, the Kibei established their own radio propaganda to weaken Japanese morale and expedite surrender.

For all their worth to the war effort, the Nisei, caught in the U.S. dilemma of need for expertise but doubts concerning loyalty, remained in limbo. They rebelled at their families' incarceration and protested the army's refusal to recognize Buddhism as a religion. When President Roosevelt visited a Kansas boot camp, the Nisei were held on the periphery at gunpoint until the President was safely out of harm's way. On the battlefield, the Nisei overachieved because of a need to prove manhood, loyalty, and racial dignity. Officers kept Nisei soldiers together lest they be shot, accidentally or intentionally, by American fire. General Douglas MacArthur, who depended on Japanese-American aides during his negotiations with the Japanese high command, also kept Nisei intelligence officers close at hand during the tense days of disarmament.

At the end of the war, Nisei accomplishments went unsung. As demonstrated by a shameful incident in Hood River, Oregon, their names were censored from reports, honor rolls, public monuments, and recommendations for medals. They received no credit for shortening the war and saving lives. Although they were constantly in danger of being captured and tortured by the enemy, the Nisei proved to be superior linguists, sensitive interrogators, dependable leaders, and cunning improvisers. Without their humane intervention on Saipan, many civilians would have committed suicide to escape what they envisioned to be a dangerous insurgency of vengeful all-white American soldiers.

The Aftermath. The internment problem did not end with camp closures or the armistice with Japan, which was signed aboard the U.S.S. *Missouri* on August 15, 1945. Japanese Americans encountered a struggle in the marketplace as well as on the street. Returning without homes, businesses, or cash, many were destitute. They were also confronted by a Caucasian mindset that anyone with stereotypically Oriental features and a Japanese surname was suspect and therefore open game for prejudicial actions and harassment. In addition to the internees' fears and disillusion, families also faced the return of veterans, who reunited with their families at internment camps as though they were visiting prison inmates. Officially expunged September 4, 1975, as a gesture to outcries from internees, their children, Asian-American legislators, and other victims of racist injustice, Executive Order 9066 appeared to be a dead issue thirty-three years after the fact.

It was not until 1981 that Attorney Peter Irons began a rectifying process. Following disclosure of government documents attesting to the fact that Roosevelt's cabinet and the FBI were well aware that Japanese Americans had posed no threat, Irons pressed for national acknowledgement that the internment camps were a blatant denial of civil rights. The suppression of evidence exonerating internees from suspicion of disloyalty, espionage, or sabotage brought Gordon Hirabayashi back to the same courtroom, only this time flanked by sixty lawyers and Japanese-American supporters. Charging the U.S. government with misconduct and proclaiming that "ancestry is not a crime," Hirabayashi held firm to his rights until February 10, 1986, when he was cleared of guilt for refusing curfew and internment.

A BRIEF SYNOPSIS

Beginning with a foreword and a time line, *Farewell to Manzanar* contains an autobiographical **memoir** of Jeanne Wakatsuki Houston's wartime incarceration at Manzanar, a Japanese-American internment camp. On Sunday, December 7, 1941, in Long Beach, California, the family—consisting of both parents, Jeanne's four brothers and five sisters, and Granny—are startled by news that Japan has attacked Pearl Harbor, Hawaii. FBI agents arrest Jeanne's father, Ko, for allegedly supplying oil to Japanese submarines and imprison him at Fort Lincoln, near Bismarck, North Dakota.

In February 1942, President Roosevelt issues Executive Order 9066 ordering Japanese-Americans to evacuate their homes and take up residence in internment camps. The Wakatsukis, with Jeanne's brother Woody at the head, are transported to Owens Valley, California, home of 10,000 internees. The family, overcrowded and miserable in Block 16, endures unappetizing institutional food, dust storms, diarrhea, lack of privacy, foul toilets, and annoying, impersonal red tape.

After his reunion with his family in September 1942, Ko escapes feelings of humiliation through the consumption of homemade rice wine and becomes an angry, bitter, drunken recluse. Jeanne avoids family disorder by hiding under the bed, studying catechism, playing hopscotch, and learning ballet. In spring 1943, the family locates better accommodations at Block 28, where Ko develops optimism through cultivating pear trees. Jeanne enjoys normal school experiences, including participation in glee club and yearbook activities.

Camp life grows difficult as a result of pro-Japanese riots and forced loyalty oaths. Many young men, including Woody, disagree with the older generation and sign up for the military as a means of proving their loyalty. Later, to prove his sense of manhood, Ko rejects leaving Manzanar in a bus and returns his clan two hundred and twenty-five miles to Long Beach via three round trips in a blue, used Nash automobile. The family locates an apartment in Cabrillo Homes, a flimsy housing project in west Long Beach. Mama works in a fish cannery; Ko is unable to find work commensurate with his need for self-esteem.

In 1951, the family moves to the Santa Clara Valley, where Ko returns to farming and raises strawberries. Jeanne rebels against Ko's strict traditionalism by serving as a majorette and being elected homecoming queen. The first Wakatsuki to gain a college degree, she marries James D. Houston, a Caucasian. In April 1972, thirty years after her family's humiliation and loss of livelihood, Jeanne Houston takes her three children to visit the skeletal remains of Manzanar. Her memories return to her father and his defiance of the racist edict that cost the family their home, business, and belongings.

LIST OF CHARACTERS

Jeanne

Jeanne, the youngest of ten children and the speaker of the book, undergoes the trauma of internment along with the normal ambivalence of children toward traditional parents. A tentative, fearful seven year old at the outset of the family's resettlement, Jeanne, born in Inglewood and raised in Ocean Park and Terminal Island, adapts to camp life by satisfying intellectual curiosity and staying active. A daddy's girl, she suffers a love-hate relationship with Ko and must cope with his alcoholism and his outrageous macho behavior. In adulthood, she patterns her own individuality after his rebellion and establishes herself as a majorette and beauty queen.

Ko (Papa) Wakatsuki

A six-footer with a military school background, Ko, a former cook, laborer, lumberjack, and government translator, is possessed of dignity and pride in his Samurai background, his ten children, and a thriving fishing business. He precedes the agents who arrest him and returns from prison with a swagger stick and self-satisfied air, yet suffers his whole life from an inability to complete what he begins. When freedom comes to Manzanar, Ko is reluctant to return to predominantly Caucasian society, and so declines to join those of his children who settle in New Jersey. In Los Angeles, he pursues a pipe dream of building a housing project with Japanese labor and allows his wife to support the family on factory wages.

Mama

A stereotypical partridge-shaped mother figure, Mrs. Wakatsuki, a Hawaiian-born beauty in her youth, attempts to hide wartime concerns from her children, but her temper explodes when a second-hand dealer tries to buy her china for $15, prior to the departure for Boyle Heights. Her decision to smash the twelve place settings indicates her doughty courage. At Manzanar, she puts to use her skill as a dietician. Returned to freedom, she locates a cannery job like the one she held at Long Beach before the war and takes Jeanne's side in family arguments about how young girls should behave.

Woody

One of the two Wakatsuki sons who assist Papa on *The Nereid*, twenty-four-year-old Woody, Ko's second oldest child, serves as a cheerful, pragmatic surrogate father during the evacuation of Terminal Island and takes a job as a carpenter. The family bulwark in Ko's absence, Woody remains determined to prove his loyalty by serving in the military in 1944. His pilgrimage to the remnants of the Wakatsuki family still in Japan, conducted while he performs peacetime duty as provisions manager and deterrent to the black market, discloses an aspect of Ko's former life that Woody had been unable to appreciate in California.

Granny

Mrs. Wakatsuki's mother, a sixty-five-year-old Japanese native who is nearly blind and too feeble to hustle for food in the mess hall, receives her food in the barracks. She never learns English and prizes the lacquerware and porcelain which came from her native land.

Chizu

Woody's wife, who comes to the pier on Sunday, December 7, 1941, to announce the Japanese attack on Pearl Harbor. Later at Manzanar, Chizu, mother of a daughter and a camp-born son named George, is a faithful daughter-in-law and peacemaker who serves the extended family as an extra mother for Jeanne and the younger Wakatsukis.

Kaz

The husband of Jeanne's sister Martha, Kaz, who is a foreman of a reservoir maintenance team at Manzanar, leads his crew on a routine inspection the night of the riot. MPs burst in on the chlorine shed and hold the men at gunpoint until they can determine why Kaz's crew would be occupying a building on the camp periphery and arming themselves with ax handles.

May

Jeanne's eleven-year-old sister who carries meals to Granny in the barracks.

Ray

At thirteen, Ray makes a game of eating in multiple mess halls. His normal behavior reflects a child's need to play, even if the playground is an internment camp.

Kiyo

Eleven-year-old Kiyo attempts to halt Ko's spouse abuse and intimidation of the family by punching his father in the face. For his courage, Kiyo earns his father's respect.

Toyo

Ko's sprightly, dignified eighty-year-old aunt, who rejoices in 1946 to learn that Ko did not die in 1913; she presents Woody a valuable silk coverlet, even though her home displays mostly bare rooms and humble woven mats. Woody learns that Toyo was the favorite aunt who provided Ko, her favorite nephew, the money to emigrate to Hawaii. Toyo sits by Woody as he sleeps and weeps at his resemblance to the Wakatsukis.

Fred Tayama

Leader of the Japanese-American Citizens League, he is badly mauled by six hostile pro-Japanese on December 5, 1942.

Joe Kurihara

A Hawaiian-born World War I veteran and riot leader who wants to renounce his citizenship and emigrate to Japan.

Sister Bernadette

An adamant Canadian-Japanese Maryknoll nun who comes to Block 28 to discuss with Ko Jeanne's wish to convert to Catholicism. Sister Bernadette is insistent enough to face down the testy father and debate the matter one on one.

Radine

A pretty blond in Jeanne's sixth grade class, she, like her classmates, is surprised to learn that Japanese Americans can speak English. It is Radine who delivers the painful news that Jeanne is not welcome in Girl Scouts and forms a pre-teen friendship which survives some of Jeanne's encounters with racism. For Jeanne, Radine epitomizes the sexual appeal of the American girl.

Leonard Rodriguez

A savvy Hispanic schoolmate, Leonard discloses the teachers' plot to alter the ballots so that Lois Carson, instead of Jeanne, will be crowned carnival queen. His loyalty to Jeanne enables her to win the title.

24

CHRONOLOGY

1904	Ko Wakatsuki immigrates from Japan to Honolulu, then accepts passage to Idaho to work as a houseboy.
1906	Mama and Granny immigrate from Hawaii to Spokane, Washington.
April 18, 1906	San Francisco suffers a cataclysmic earthquake and fire the day before Mama and Granny arrive.
1909	Ko enters the University of Idaho to study law.
1915	Ko elopes with Mama.
1934	Jeanne Wakatsuki, the youngest of ten children, is born in Inglewood, California.
December 21, 1941	Ko Wakatsuki is arrested by FBI agents following the bombing of Pearl Harbor.
Winter 1941-42	Ko suffers from alcohol abuse and frostbite in both feet during imprisonment at Fort Lincoln, North Dakota.
February 25, 1942	The fatherless Wakatsukis are ordered to vacate Terminal Island because the government fears that Japanese Americans threaten the naval base.
April 1942	Twelve Wakatsukis move from Boyle Heights in Los Angeles to Manzanar and settle in Block 16 of the barracks. Mitsue Endo challenges her detention at Topaz Camp, Utah.
June 10, 1942	Wada and crew dedicate Manzanar's flagpole circle.
September 1942	Chizu gives birth to George, Ko's first grandson, the day before Ko returns from prison. Ko is labeled an *inu*, or collaborator.
December 1942	Militant pro-Japanese dissidents organize a camp riot. Camp officials provide families with Christmas trees.
February 1943	Internees are forced to sign a loyalty oath to honor the U.S. and serve in the military if called to do so.
Spring 1943	The Wakatsukis move to more bearable quar-

ters in Block 28. Ko takes up gardening and prunes pear trees. Eleanor gives birth to a son while her husband, Shig, serves in the military.

August 1944 — Woody is drafted.

November 1944 — Woody is called up for active duty in Germany.

Winter 1944 — Only 6,000 internees remain at Manzanar.

January 1945 — Internees begin returning to homes and farms.

June 1945 — The Manzanar high school publishes a second yearbook, *Valediction 1945*. The camp's schools close.

August 6, 1945 — The war ends following the dropping of an atomic bomb on Hiroshima, Japan.

Early October, 1945 — The Wakatsukis depart Manzanar, leaving 2,000 internees behind. They settle in Cabrillo Homes in Long Beach.

December 1, 1945 — Internment camps close.

1951 — Ko moves his family to a strawberry farm in San Jose.

1957 — Ko dies.

1965 — Mama Wakatsuki dies.

1966 — Jeanne Houston, still emotionally affected by internment, cannot make herself speak to a Caucasian woman who worked as a Manzanar photographer.

April 1972 — Jeanne and James Houston drive their three children from Santa Cruz to Manzanar.

CRITICAL COMMENTARIES

FOREWORD

Dedicated to Ko, Riku, and Woody Wakatsuki, *A Farewell to Manzanar* opens with a straightforward **statement of purpose**: speaking for herself and her husband, Jeanne Wakatsuki Houston, intent on publicizing a racial injustice after twenty-five years of repression, links the event with concentration camps in Poland and

Siberia, then contrasts these lethal hellholes with the semi-civilized, city-like atmosphere of Manzanar, with its high school yearbook, judo pavilion, and barracks. Even with these amenities and activities, however, the specter of incarceration remains in guard towers which dot the perimeter. The Houstons' objectivity sets a **detached tone** in the two-page chronology, which covers the Japanese experience in America from 1869, when immigrants first settled the California mainland. The list continues in time order through internment, release, end of World War II, and passage of the naturalization law in 1952. The authors define three crucial terms:

- **Issei** [ee' say] people like Ko and Granny, who immigrate from Japan to the U.S.

- **Nisei** [nee' say] children like Jeanne Wakatsuki and her siblings, who are born in the U. S. to Issei parents

- **Sansei** [san' say] the third generation of Japanese Americans, like the Wakatsuki grandchildren, who were born during and after World War II, some delivered in the Manzanar hospital.

This clarification introduces a crucial theme: the varied **points of view** and responses of Japanese Americans, depending upon where and when they were born and their connection with Japan, its language, religion, and traditions.

Almost like a **coda**, the quotation by American historian and educator Henry Steele Commager emphasizes the futility and waste of Executive Order 9066 by noting that no one uncovered "a single case of Japanese disloyalty or sabotage during the whole war." On a more personal note, the quotation of Thich Nhat Hanh's **lyric verse** links Jeanne's experience with all people who locate their place in history.

Part I

CHAPTER 1

Summary

Set on a warm day at Terminal Island in Long Beach, California, on Sunday the 7th, the first weekend in December 1941, Jeanne, the **first-person** narrator, watches the Wakatsuki family's fishing boat, *The Nereid*, chug out to sea then inexplicably turn back and return to the pier. Unable to fathom why the boat is returning to Terminal Island, the family learns from a cannery worker that Japan has attacked Pearl Harbor, Hawaii. That night, Papa burns a Japanese flag and documents which connect him with Japan, from which he emigrated in 1906. Two weeks later, he is arrested. According to a Santa Monica newspaper, Papa was arrested for allegedly delivering oil to Japanese submarines. Jeanne does not see her father again for a year.

Commentary

From the outset, the authors establish a normal atmosphere consistent with the lives of all residents of coastal California. A number of details connect the Wakatsuki family with other Americans.

- Papa, a proud, hard-working entrepreneur, runs two boats in hopes of paying off his debt to the cannery from a percentage of earned profit.

- Like most citizens who heard the news on December 7, 1941, Mama is unfamiliar with Pearl Harbor.

- The author stresses a subtle link to the American Revolution by comparing the cannery worker to Paul Revere, a near-**legendary** figure who rode horseback to warn rural patriots that the British were about to attack the colonists.

To lessen the harshness of FBI paranoia, Jeanne comments diplomatically that agents were "sworn in hastily during the turbulent days right after Pearl Harbor." But, like children everywhere, Jeanne is alarmed that her father, the family's anchor, has disappeared from their lives.

(Here and in the following sections, difficult words and phrases are translated for you, as are those below.)

- *Nereid*   in Greek mythology, a sea nymph.

- **Terminal Island**   a coastal ghetto extending from Long beach and dominated by French's and Van Camp's canneries. The outer edge of Terminal Island houses the Long Beach Naval Shipyard.

- **alien**   a resident of a foreign country whose status is determined by the government bureaucracy, which can deport undesirables without recourse to courts.

• **saboteur** Government officials fear that Japanese Americans will revive loyalties to Japan and hinder the United States' war effort through violent or destructive acts, such as blowing up dams or power plants or destroying planes or ships.

CHAPTERS 2–4

Summary

In her brief **recap**, or summary, of family history, Jeanne recalls that her father early instilled a fear of Oriental people—particularly, Chinese. After Papa's arrest and the family's move from Ocean Park to a shack on Terminal Island, where Mama and Woody's wife Chizu work in a cannery, Jeanne is terrified of an Oriental-looking Caucasian girl in her kindergarten class. The family remains on Terminal Island until February 25, 1942, when all Orientals are removed to prevent potential danger to the Long Beach Naval Station. Quakers help the Wakatsukis—Mama, sixty-five-year-old Granny, older brother Woody and his wife Chizu, Bill, Kiyo, May, and Jeanne—move to Boyle Heights in Los Angeles. Already, President Roosevelt's Executive Order 9066 authorizes discretionary resettlement of Japanese Americans.

Numbered and tagged like luggage, Jeanne boards a Greyhound bus with many relatives and travels to Owens Valley, then through barbed wire to the internment camp, and finally, to their two units of Block 16, the new home for the twelve-member family. Jeanne, the youngest, delights in being so far from home and enjoys sharing a bed with Mama. The next morning, Woody optimistically oversees the sealing of knotholes to keep out desert dust, which powders the family like flour. Angered by the drafty, spartan accommodations, Mama comments, "Animals live like this."

Commentary

Jeanne's **narrative** reveals her insecurity among roughneck, streetwise kids, an unease exacerbated by her unfamiliarity with the Japanese language. A change in schools, unsettling to any young child, introduces her to the beginning of a pattern of anti-Asian sentiment from her Boyle Heights teacher, who rejects her. The eventual move to Manzanar, in Jeanne's estimation, seems almost a relief because it distances Japanese Americans from racist attacks. Jeanne sums up the tenuous state of affairs in a single sentence: "They were as frightened of the Caucasians as Caucasians were of us."

Among internees, Jeanne, an exuberant child who is obviously too young to muster outrage or bitterness, yells from the window of the bus as it arrives at Owens Valley, "Hey! This whole bus is full of Wakatsukis!" Later, she laughs at olive-drab government issue earmuffs, caps, peacoats, and leggings left over from World War I. To her, the family looks clownish in oversized GI attire. Her humor dims, however, as chronic diarrhea from typhoid shots and spoiled food sends her to foul latrines. Meaningful **details**, such as the need for cardboard shields around toilets and blankets to separate beds, demonstrate the repugnance that fastidious Japanese women feel as a result of their undeserved privations. The belief that "it can't be helped" and the courtesy with which they respect each other delineate deeply ingrained survivalism which makes life bearable in the desert camp.

- **Kyushu**   Japan's deep south, the southernmost of the four major islands in the island chain.

- **Samurai**   a member of a warrior class one grade lower than nobility, whose ancestry dates to feudal Japan.

- **American Friends Service**   a Quaker charitable organization founded in 1917 and awarded the Nobel Peace Prize in 1947.

- **Executive Order**   an edict resulting from the discretionary powers of the president, who, as commander in chief of the U.S. military, may legally suspend citizen rights during wartime in the interests of national security.

- **internment**   confinement as a method of assuring that no anti-American effort can be carried out by potential Japanese aggressors.

- **Charlie Chaplin**   a popular silent movie comic of the 1920s and 1930s.

CHAPTERS 5–7

Summary

The Wakatsuki family begins to fragment as older members

take meager money-making jobs in the camp, and Jeanne turns to peer activities and people wanting entertainment. Lacking home religious instruction, she is attracted to a new type of stability: nuns who run a children's village. Gruesome stories of Christian saints and martyrs keep Jeanne interested in the local chapel, which is a mile from her barracks. Walking through 100 degree heat brings on sunstroke, which keeps her in bed for a week. In September 1942, Papa Ko, looking ten years older, returns from Fort Lincoln, a prison southeast of Bismark, North Dakota. Chapter 7 reconstructs the interrogations which initiated Ko's imprisonment.

Commentary

Much of Jeanne's **commentary** reveals scholarly grounding in sociological research. In evaluating the damage done to families, she concludes, "My own family, after three years of mess hall living, collapsed as an integrated unit." In Manzanar, she yearned for the early years when her family shared abundant meals at a great round table in their Ocean Park home. Eventually, authorities perceive the importance to a family unit of shared meals. From that point on, internees are encouraged to dine in intimate, supportive family groups, but their efforts are too late.

The **narrative** recounts Papa's return, then segues back into his history as a strongly individualistic teenager grown into an entrepreneur and autocratic father. The experience of internment and separation from Ko forces Jeanne into soul-wrenching evaluations of his character and behavior. She concludes as generously as the facts allow with a brief analytic **character sketch**:

> He was not a great man. He wasn't even a very successful man. He was a poser, a braggart, and a tyrant. But he had held onto his self-respect, he dreamed grand dreams, and he could work well at any task he turned his hand to: he could raise vegetables, sail a boat, plead a case in small claims court, sing Japanese poems, make false teeth, carve a pig.

The severity of Jeanne's estimation suggests the high cost of so scathing an evaluation of her highly valued father. To redeem her father, she recreates a prison scene with a twenty-nine-year-old interrogator in which Ko demonstrates his **humanism** by saying:

"As long as military men control the country you are always going to have a war."

- **grunion** silver fish the size of sardines which swim ashore in high tide to spawn in wet sand at the full of the moon and are caught by hand or in a net.

- **kabuki** a popular, stylized Japanese theater performance featuring melodramatic colorful costumes, wigs, makeup, posturing, singing, and dancing.

- **Maryknoll** the popular name for the Catholic Foreign Mission Society of America.

- **catechism** a specified list of questions and answers which teaches the principles of Catholicism.

- **swagger stick** a metal-tipped baton carried by military officers as a symbol of authority.

- **Commodore Perry** an American naval officer who opened Japan's ports to Westerners.

- **Miya-jima** an island twelve miles south of the city of Hiroshima.

- **Niigata** a coastal city on the island of Honshu about 100 miles north of Tokyo.

- *Nippon* Japanese for "Japan."

- **Ty Cobb** A famed outfielder and base stealer for the Detroit Tigers from 1905 to 1926, he was the first baseball star honored at the Baseball Hall of Fame in Cooperstown, New York.

- **Wakatsuki Ko** Using her father's full name, the author illustrates the Oriental practice of placing the family name before the given name.

CHAPTERS 8–11

Summary

In the **rising action**, life becomes more complex, more disordered for the Wakatsukis after Ko returns. Disturbed by imprisonment, he paces about the barracks, refuses to go outside, and uses spare rice or syrupy fruit to distill home-brewed wine. Because internees suspect him of informing on Japanese loyalists in order to end his imprisonment in North Dakota, they call him *inu*, which means both "dog" and "collaborator." Ko, an egotistical man incapable of coping with humiliation, lapses into alcoholism, self-exile, uncontrolled bouts of anger, exasperating tantrums, and wife abuse. After Ko menaces his wife, eleven-year-old Kiyo steps between them and punches his father in the face, then flees to his sister's quarters to hide.

Jeanne acknowledges that Ko's spiritual and economic emasculation reflects the powerlessness of all male internees. As she summarizes Ko's impotence: "He had no rights, no home, no control over his own life." By December, the first anniversary of the attack on Pearl Harbor, the camp erupts in violent rioting as 2,000 malcontents roam the camp singing Japanese songs and mouthing threats at MPs. Two Japanese youths are shot to death, others injured. The new camp director lamely makes amends for the event by providing families with Christmas trees.

In February 1943, polarization continues with the forced loyalty oath which requires internees to state their allegiance to the U.S. and their willingness to serve in the armed forces. Ko abandons his self-imposed isolation as he is drawn into debates with other male internees and into intense arguments with Woody, who wants an opportunity to prove his loyalty by joining the U.S. army. A footnote attests to the logic of Woody and his peers, who form the all-Nisei 442nd Regiment, "the most decorated American unit in World War II; it also suffered the highest percentage of casualties and deaths." Such **overcompensation** suggests the tremendous psychic pressures that a war with Japan placed on Japanese Americans.

The multi-faceted **dilemma** of which blanks to check "yes" or "no" forces Ko into sobriety. Clean-shaven and again proud to head a household, he limps away to the mess hall. By 4:00 P.M., as Jeanne plays hopscotch, the men's discussion ends with Ko tackling a fleeing man who called him a collaborator. Others intervene to keep Ko from strangling his attacker. At this section's **climax**, the night ends with a sandstorm and the family clustered near the oil stove, where Woody, Chizu, and Mama listen to Ko and a female friend of Woody's wife sing *Kimi ga yo*, the Japanese national anthem, which Jeanne characterizes as a "personal **credo** for endurance."

Commentary

Jeanne, maintaining the **point of view** of a young child, recalls the riot peripherally because she is too young to take part. Her game of hopscotch, a universal pastime, **symbolizes** her need to keep moving in incremental steps toward an attainable goal. As demonstrated later by her interest in dancing, singing, and baton twirling, Jeanne has a need to act out her frustrations with vigorous physical play, which relieves her of the stress of thinking too much about mature political and ideological debate, which she is too young to understand.

The adult **conflict**, an ideological debate between extremist males, results in confrontations with armed military police, tear gas, and gunfire. Although two men die in the fray, Jeanne recalls her **sensory impressions** of ringing bells and searchlights, "making shadows ebb and flow among the barracks like dark, square waves." Chapter 10, an **interpolated episode**, shifts point of view to Kaz, Jeanne's brother-in-law, who, along with other reservoir crewmen, encounters wild-eyed MPs swinging tommy guns and shouting "Japs" at men whom they assume to be saboteurs. The scene stresses an **axiom** of imprisonment—guards are drawn into the violence and paranoia that they create and thus become victims themselves.

The loyalty oath evolves into a crucible in which the true mettle of citizenship is determined. As Jeanne describes it, the dilemma for Japanese Americans is a circle with three exits: "The first led into the infantry, the second back across the Pacific. The third, called *relocation* . . . " The latter choice would result in transport to the Tule Lake repatriation camp, from which the disloyal were to be sent back to Japan. Any of the choices threatens cataclysm for Japanese families, who have come to think of Manzanar as a refuge, despite its inconveniences and barbaric amenities.

The **catharsis** wrought during the sandstorm allows Jeanne to accept Ko as a beleaguered adult. In her view, he is unable to resolve the political forces that buffet him and therefore takes temporary refuge in a childhood **credo** and in tears. The line of the Japanese national anthem which refers to the flowering lichen that coats the rock **foreshadows** Ko's eventual refuge in gardening, a traditional outlet which absorbs his energies and restores beauty to his fragmented life.

- **banzai** a Japanese interjection which serves as greeting, battle cry, or cheer and translates "May you live ten thousand years!"

- **samisen** a three-string Japanese banjo.

Part II

CHAPTERS 12-14

Summary

By spring 1943, as families relocate, barracks begin to empty. The twelve Wakatsukis move to Block 28, which is more convenient to Mama's job as dietician at the hospital. Ko develops an interest in a neglected pear orchard, succulent gardening, painting, sketching, and making furniture from myrtle limbs. The family, with double the space they once shared, is able to create a more liveable environment by installing Sheetrock. Tight security is eased to allow for walks along the base of the Sierra Mountains. Ko takes spiritual comfort in Mt. Whitney, which resembles Fujiyama in Japan.

At Woody's insistence, the family comes to accept internment as a situation which cannot be changed, one which must be endured. Other residents make the best of their incarceration by taking advantage of "schools, churches, Boy Scouts, beauty parlors, neighborhood gossip, fire and police departments, glee clubs, softball leagues, Abbott and Costello movies, tennis courts, and traveling shows." Ironically, remaining in camp appears much less problematic than returning to a neighborhood where anti-Japanese feeling may curtail the freedoms they enjoy at Manzanar.

Jeanne, who at age ten is understandably "desperate to be 'accepted,'" embraces fourth grade activities, including girls' glee club, an overnight camping trip, and baton twirling. An aged geisha attempts to teach her the traditional Japanese skill of *odori*, the stylized dance performed in **kabuki drama**, but Jeanne opts for ballet, which proves as disappointing as lessons from the old geisha. Casting about for some kind of activity to absorb her energies, Jeanne returns to the Maryknoll nuns and studies catechism, not so much for spiritual enlightenment or grace as for the attention received by converts. Ko, of a different mind on the matter of conversion, forbids Jeanne's religious choice on the grounds that she will never find a Japanese Catholic to marry. Following a threatening, potential stalemate between Ko and Sister Bernadette, Jeanne accepts defeat and sublimates her hatred of parental authority by tossing her baton, a **symbol** of her autocratic father. In her words, "I would throw him into the air and watch him twirl, and catch him, and throw him high, again and again and again."

Jeanne eventually realizes that Ko was right to forbid acceptance of Catholic beliefs, mainly because she was too immature to understand the ramifications of her choice. The return of her oldest sister, Eleanor, diverts family attention to life-threatening problems. While Eleanor's husband, Shig, fights in Germany with the American infantry, she voluntarily reenters Manzanar for the last months of her pregnancy. The family is relieved when the boy baby arrives and both child and mother survive. For a change, Ko and his wife embrace, weeping in a shared love of family.

Commentary

This section comprises the **falling action**, the coming together and meshing of forces which had been at odds. After suffering months of displacement, the Wakatsukis acquire a makeshift contentment. In nature, Ko takes temporary refuge from the dilemma of which of the two warring governments is right and which nation—Japan or the U.S.—claims the greatest share of his soul. As Jeanne describes the inspiration of Mount Whitney, it "represented those forces in nature, those powerful and inevitable forces that cannot be resisted, reminding a man that sometimes he must simply endure that which cannot be changed."

The **irony** of the name Manzanar, Spanish for "apple orchard," echoes the invigorating forces of nature which replenish spirits and restore interest in life. Like prisoners, internees turn to "the little bit of busywork you had right in front of you, [which] became the most urgent thing." Sublimating despair and rage, the simple will to go on keeps Mama immersed in the dietary needs of her neighbors, Papa puttering at his hobbies, and the Wakatsuki boys interested in arrowheads, football, a hillbilly band, and a dance band.

The authors return to the **theme** of American normality, which is captured in the music and yearnings of kids who resemble teens outside internment camp fences. Twirling batons, jitterbugging to "Don't Fence Me In," a popular tune of the era, and singing "Beautiful Dreamer," "Down by the Old Mill Stream," "Shine on, Harvest Moon," and "Battle Hymn of the Republic," young people who would have graduated from schools named "Theodore Roosevelt, Thomas Jefferson, Herbert Hoover, Sacred Heart" complete their education in camp. All the members of the fictional McIntyre family, which is the focus of the school play, *Growing Pains*, have Caucasian names, but are played by Oriental students named Shoji Katayama, Takudo Ando, and Kazuko Nagai. Jeanne, by this time old enough to envy older kids, thumbs the pages of *Our World*, the 1943–1944 yearbook, picturing "school kids with armloads of books, wearing cardigan sweaters and walking past rows of tarpapered shacks."

A minuscule **subplot** features a Quaker volunteer named Lois and her sweetheart, Isao, in a star-crossed Romeo and Juliet romance. Like young lovers everywhere, the pair waits until juvenile campers are asleep before withdrawing to the privacy of the desert. A romantic at heart, Jeanne comments, "It was years later that I remembered and understood what that outing must have been for them." As proved in the Dr. Seuss tale *How the Grinch Stole Christmas*, the joy and mystery of growing up and discovering love, just like Christmas in Whoville, arrives on time in its traditional form, even though the populace is immured behind barbed wire and scrutinized from watchtowers that sweep the rows of barracks with searchlights. In their tireless searches, the floodlights disclose no subversives—only ordinary people doing ordinary things.

- **sake** (sah′ kee)   Japanese rice wine.

- **succulents**   fleshy, juice-filled plants, sometimes called "living stones."

- **Fujiyama**   a snow-capped mountain in Japan which resembles Mount Whitney, a large mountain overlooking Owens Valley, California.

- **obsidian**   volcanic glass which holds a lethal edge and was prized by prehistoric weapon makers for arrowheads.

- **Jive Bombers**   a swing dance band named with a pun on dive bombers, reminiscent of the notorious kamikaze, or suicide bombers, who deliberately crashed planes onto the decks of American ships.

- **judo**   a technique of self-defense, using no weapons.

- **kendo**   dueling with bamboo swords.

- **geisha**   a Japanese woman trained to entertain men by engaging in pleasant conversation, singing, dancing, and playing stringed instruments. Geishas should not be confused with either waitresses or prostitutes. Their profession was highly respected and required punctilious training in grace, charm, and deportment.

- **firebreak**   an artificial barrier or plowed strip which halts the spread of fire. Firebreaks were essential to wooden camps where barracks were built so close together that desert winds could easily spread fire.

- **tatami mats**   traditional woven straw mats used as area rugs.

- **chignon**   a French twist, an arrangement that pulls hair sleekly to the side of the head and into a tight knot at the back.

- **Wakatsuki-san**   the combination of a name and a respectful title—for example, Mr. Wakatsuki, sir.

CHAPTERS 15–17

Summary

Relaxation of anti-Japanese government policies allows more people to leave Manzanar. With only 6,000 remaining at the end of 1944, the leaving of Eleanor, Shig, and the baby, as well as Woody's conscription into the army in August, create gaps in Jeanne's family. Two plaintiffs—Gordon Hirabayashi and Fred Korematsu—fail to force the government to rescind racist laws. Pressed by a third, Mitsue Endo, a successful challenge to racial exclusion results in a landmark decision from the high court: "The government cannot detain loyal citizens against their will." Within twelve months, detainment ceases and detainees begin to return to their homes as the Western Defense Command begins to close internment camps.

Release brings mixed feelings. With no home to return to, the Wakatsukis are ambivalent about their new freedom to live again among racists whose "wartime propaganda—racist headlines, atrocity movies, hate slogans, and fright-mask posters—had turned the Japanese face into something despicable and grotesque." The imminent departure, freighted with the humiliation of three years' of unjust confinement, puts Jeanne in touch with an indefinable ache which she terms "the foretaste of being hated." Rather than confront California-style racism, Jeanne's older sisters and brothers choose to move east to New Jersey.

Ko, of a different generation, continues to think of the West Coast as his home and, as diffident as a slave freed during the Civil War, sticks to the old way of life "out of habit or lethargy or fear." Since he can no longer hold a commercial fishing license and his boats and nets have been either confiscated, repossessed, or stolen, he chooses to let the government reinstate him in public life and commerce. At the hospital, Mama observes rampant psychosomatic aches and pains among internees, indicative of insecurity and hesitancy to leave Manzanar. To ease tightness in Mama's back, Jeanne *momos* (massages) the knotted muscles.

Meanwhile, Ko, in response to a need for housing, proposes a cooperative through which Japanese men will build a housing project in which to settle internees. The departure date looms as summer ends. In August, an atomic bomb incinerates Hiroshima.

By now, the once tightly knit Wakatuski family has, like the camp, deteriorated. Woody is in the army at Fort Douglas, Utah; Eleanor lives in Reno; her husband is stationed in Germany with the occupation troops; Bill and Martha and Frances and Lillian are living in New Jersey; and Ray is now in the Coast Guard, the only service that would take him at the age of seventeen.

In early October, the remaining Wakatsukis can no longer postpone departure.

Commentary

The **paradox** of internment stands out in bold relief as the days of internment draw to a close. The victims of unjust detainment are understandably reluctant to return to San Diego, Los Angeles, and San Francisco, cities where they once lived in peace. With racist groups like No Japs Incorporated, Home Front Commandos, and the Pacific Coast Japanese Problem League already preparing a hostile welcome, Asians tended to cling to the artificial security of Manzanar. Long accused of clannishness and refusal to assimilate, Japanese Americans, after three years of living in a "desert ghetto," feared a return to wartime animosities, marked by assaults, arson, and KKK-style nightriders with shotguns.

In a skillful mating of Americana and **incongruity**, Jeanne notes, "All the truly good things, it often seemed, the things we couldn't get, were outside, and had to be sent for, or shipped in. In this sense, God and the Sears, Roebuck catalogue were pretty much one and the same in my young mind." Intent on testing her faith by challenging God's generosity, she prays devoutly for nine days for apricots, which fail to arrive. No longer assured that a beneficent deity answers prayer, she returns to a faith in Sears, Roebuck and "*the outside*, where all such good things could be found."

Farewell to Manzanar Genealogy
and
Illustrative Maps

Ko's g
(a judge of tl

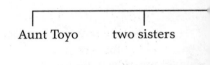

Aunt Toyo	two sisters

Granny

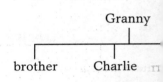

brother	Charlie

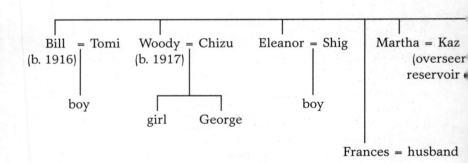

Bill = Tomi (b. 1916)	Woody = Chizu (b. 1917)	Eleanor = Shig	Martha = Kaz (overseer reservoir
boy		boy	
	girl　George		

Frances = husband

= married to
• engaged to

nar **Genealogy**

father
murai class)

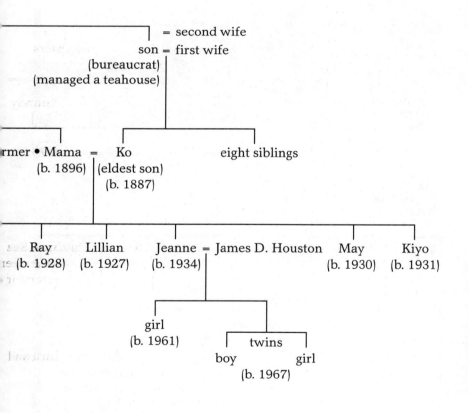

```
                              ┌─── = second wife
                        son ─ = first wife
                   (bureaucrat)
              (managed a teahouse)

rmer • Mama  =   Ko              eight siblings
     (b. 1896) │(eldest son)
               │ (b. 1887)

  Ray      Lillian     Jeanne = James D. Houston   May      Kiyo
(b. 1928) (b. 1927)   (b. 1934)                  (b. 1930) (b. 1931)

                      girl
                    (b. 1961)      twins
                               boy      girl
                                (b. 1967)
```

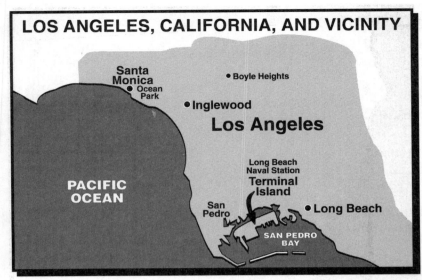

Much of the Wakatsuki family history centers around the Long Beach area. In pre–World War II contentment, they captured grunion on the beach near the cannery where Jeanne's mother worked and the pier where Ko and his sons operated a profitable fishing business. After internment, the family returned to Long Beach and lived in Cabrillo Homes, which sheltered a racial hodgepodge still sorting out post-war traumas.

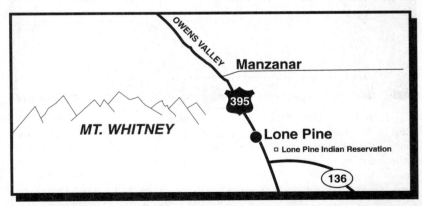

Manzanar, one of ten Japanese internment camps and the largest city between Reno and Los Angeles, perched on the north end of the Mojave Desert. A dismal square mile of dust, rattlesnakes, emptiness, and restless winds, the site lurked in Jeanne's memory until 1972, when repression could no longer shield her from loss and family shame.

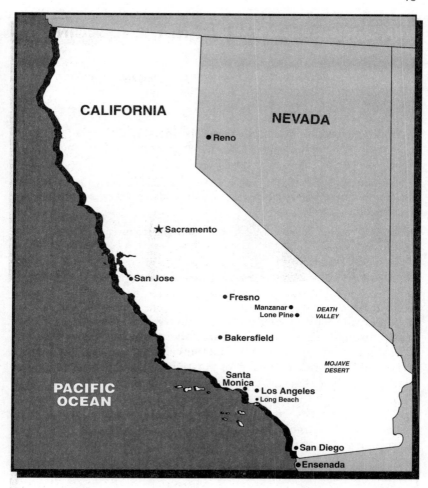

Jeanne's life centered on a California triad—a secure childhood in Long Beach, followed by wrenching turmoil after government officials transported the Wakatsuki family northeast to Manzanar, then a new start on a strawberry farm near San Jose in 1952. In the 1950s, she met James Houston at the University of San Jose and established a family. In 1972, Jeanne reversed the pattern of her family's migration by swinging south to Bakersfield, then east and north to revisit the few remnants of government barracks which once incarcerated members of her race.

- **Ex Parte Endo**   the Latin designation of Mitsuo Endo's legal case.

- **habeas corpus**   a Latin phrase meaning "let you have the body," a basic concept upon which all other freedoms rest: that American citizens are exempt from illegal or capricious detention or imprisonment.

- **rescinded**   struck down.

- **American Legion**   a confederation of honorably discharged wartime veterans. Founded in 1919, the group is comprised of more than 3,000,000 members.

- **The Native Sons of the Golden West**   a San Francisco-based men's fraternal order founded in 1875 and dedicated to preserving western history and landmarks.

- **novena**   a nine-day Catholic devotional requiring intense prayer.

CHAPTER 18

Summary

In April 1946, Woody and his eighty-year-old great aunt Toyo walk through Ka-ke, a graveyard about fifteen miles outside Hiroshima, and view the memorial tombstone which represents the Wakatsuki family's honoring of Ko, whom they unofficially declared dead in 1913. Hesitant to approach his Old Country family, Woody eases the fear of rejection by bringing fifty pounds of sugar and soon connects securely with a loving family who accept his GI crewcut and his Americanness. During the night, he awakens to the tearful face of his aunt, sitting close enough to search out his Wakatsuki facial qualities. Woody is too moved to speak, yet longs to hear more of his family's history.

Commentary

This **interlude**, printed in italics, is a departure from the fragmentation wrought by the dissolution of Manzanar's homogeneity and restores a semblance of family, of wholeness to Woody. In a country where tombstones tilt crazily from the concussion of the atomic bomb, where upper-class homes preserve a threadbare respectability despite wartime privation, a GI *Nisei*, much like Alex Haley, author of *Roots* and *Queen*, pursues his ancestry. Woody, secure in a position of strength and authority over post-war provisions management, needs no handout. He is proud of his accomplishments, yet curiously needful of acceptance and esteem. The pleasant exchanges with Toyo, his father's favorite aunt, whether spoken or wordless, produce an **apotheosis**, a dawning awareness of who he is and where he comes from. More than internal knowledge, the coming together provides him with a treasured, second-hand glimpse of his feisty, cocky father who verbally did battle with him throughout internment and refused to let go the reins of family control to an Americanized generation, one that had never known their Japanese legacy. **Symbolically**, Woody achieves his awareness while lying cocooned in restful repose, like an infant awakening in the bosom of a welcoming family. Out of respect to Ko, Woody, emotionally closed off from his aunts by "the dark, quiet maze of screens and mats and corridors," keeps to himself his perceptions. Instead of words tonight, next day, he will climb Papa's favorite hill to "see what his eyes used to see."

This drastic shift in time, place, and point of view—a recreation of the pilgrimage **motif**—provides a useful buffer, a separation from the complex worries of how to leave Manzanar, how to pick up the threads of family support, how to face once more a world dominated by the privilege and power of white skin. Woody, the only American relative among native Japanese Wakatsukis, experiences an acceptance which bodes well for the family at home in the U.S. The authors seem to be concluding that if Aunt Toyo can overlook the cataclysm of Hiroshima and weep with joy over the family's lost sheep, then Ko, Mama, Jeanne, Granny, and the others, far across the Pacific, can make similar adjustments to a new world order.

CHAPTERS 19–20

Summary

Impulsively, Ko (ever the exhibitionist) decides one day that if the Wakatsuki clan must return to the world, they will do so in style. Purchasing a "midnight blue Nash sedan" in Lone Pine, he restores his self-esteem by repatriating his family *his* way—even if it means making three trips for family members and belongings over the 225 miles from Owens Valley to Long Beach. To the surprise of Jeanne and her mother, the feared predictions of racism prove untrue. Like refugees, the Wakatsukis drop their fears of ostracism and turn to the pressing need for housing, which consists of scraps and oddments—"trailer camps, Quonset huts, back rooms of private homes, church social halls, anywhere they could fit."

Again, Quakers help them; this time, they locate an apartment in Cabrillo Homes, a government-built project in west Long Beach. Mama collects her kitchenware and silver from former neighbors in Boyle Heights; however, the warehouse which stored their furniture and appliances has been "unaccountably 'robbed.'" Without essentials, including Ko's boats, the family "[starts] over from economic zero." Reflecting on her father's losses, Jeanne, sensitive to the male achievement drive, labels them "another snip of the castrator's scissors." While Ko pursues idealistic plans of creating a Japanese housing project, Mama pragmatically applies her $500 in savings to current needs and returns to fish cannery employment.

For eleven-year-old Jeanne, an unsettling first day in school begins with an innocent gaffe—Radine, a white classmate, is surprised that Jeanne can speak English. Jeanne decides to do her best and absorb rejection by blaming herself for failure, including exclusion from Girl Scouts, a whites-only group run by snooty mothers. Undaunted by the turn-down, Jeanne and Radine become buddies; Radine rebuffs others' racist stares, Jeanne teaches her to twirl a baton. Expertise leads to Jeanne's acceptance as lead majorette with a Boy Scout drum and bugle corps, supported by a pack of admiring fathers.

Maturation forces a wedge between Jeanne and Ko, who insists that his daughter follow the female ideal of his Old Country youth rather than the American image of the late 1940s. Ruefully, she castigates herself: "I had lost respect for Papa." In the struggle to assert his masculinity, Ko joins Woody in a plan to dry and sell abalone. Initially, the venture seems hopeful, but eventually it goes "to pieces." The failure of the scheme further depletes Ko's sense of manhood as Woody assumes more importance to the family and Ko returns to alcohol, an addiction which shames and troubles Jeanne. The most crushing embarrassment comes at a PTA awards dinner where Ko, overdressed and over-formal, humiliates Jeanne by executing "a slow, deep, Japanese bow from the waist" when she is recognized for her scholastic achievement by the principal.

Commentary

The shift in **setting** is of primary importance to the remainder of the book. The return to more civilized accommodations begins with the flushing of the toilet, a welcome sound to these former internees who are used to foul-odored, stopped-up toilets and standing in line at crowded latrines that worked. The Wakatsukis rejoice in private bedrooms and a kitchen where they can cook what they choose and eat as a family. The environment, typical of government planning, consists of two-story stucco units, plank banisters, community clotheslines, and sparse landscaping. A few years later, when Jeanne is old enough to enter high school, she finally sees Cabrillo Homes for what it is: little more than "a half-finished and undermaintained army base."

A serious **theme**, the loss of status, reflects a basic difference in male and female adults. Just as post-Civil War and Depression-era unemployment emasculated black males as black females discovered the empowerment of domestic work for real wages, Papa's loss of status contrasts with Mama's return to the position of wage earner. A proud man too status conscious to join her in menial work, Ko absorbs himself in blueprints of a dream neighborhood.

For Jeanne, the battlefield of the sixth grade is tangible proof that detainment has forever labeled her as foreign, "the slant-eyed face, the Oriental." In a significant **coming-to-knowledge** of her family's ordeal, she concludes, "You cannot deport 110,000 people unless you have stopped seeing individuals." More demeaning is her awareness that she and other Orientals have acquiesced to unjust treatment out of the subconscious belief that their detainment was somehow deserved. With a child's logic, Jeanne, a pre-teen Alice in Wonderland, chooses to shrink into social invisibility, but she offsets the possibility of complete extinction by overachieving through academic performance and athletics, by participating in yearbook, newspaper, and student government, and by asserting her femininity in her gold-braided majorette costume, which displays her *gobo* legs.

- **Bismarck** the "Bismarck stick" is a pun on Bismarck, North Dakota, site of the prison where Ko was incarcerated, and on Otto von Bismarck (1815–1898), a Prussian statesman who unified Germany; he is remembered for his dandified airs as he brandished a swagger stick while he inspected troops.

- **Okie**   an insulting nickname applied to midwestern farmers who were ruined in the 1930s by the Dust Bowl. These rural down-and-outers from Oklahoma, Kansas, Texas, New Mexico, and surrounding areas packed their families and goods on tenuous antique vehicles and journeyed west to California to search out a better life for their dispossessed families. John Steinbeck immortalized the Joads, a fictional family of Okies bound for California, in *The Grapes of Wrath*, the source of a 1940 motion picture by the same name, starring Henry Fonda as Tom Joad and Jane Darwell as Ma.

- **Burma-Shave signs**   a uniquely successful advertising idea utilizing a series of small, unobtrusive roadside advertisements which formed a witty jingle.

- **Quonset huts**   a trademark name for drab, prefabricated shelters designed like long loaves of bread.

- **this is usually just another form of invisibility**   that is, seeing the female body as a sex object rather than the outer representation of a human individual.

- **abalone**   a tasty mollusk similar to scallops.

CHAPTER 21

Summary

Partnered with Radine, a poor white Texas girl attempting to rise in society, Jeanne enters Long Beach Polytechnic High School, where Radine outdistances her by being invited to join a sorority, while Jeanne is rejected as high school majorette. The two girls, similar in values, are attracted to similar boys, but it is Radine who is asked to dances. Jeanne, even before she might be invited by a likeable Caucasian, makes sure that classmates know that she is unavailable—lest she have to reject a date that would involve a meeting at the project between the white boy and her virulent, judgmental Japanese father.

In their senior year, as competition with Radine extinguishes Jeanne's hopes of popularity, Ko, forced into sobriety by a bout of vomiting blood, moves the family to the Santa Clara Valley, outside San Jose, to raise strawberries. Jeanne's longing for attention comes to fruition with the election of the annual carnival queen. Barefoot and dressed in an exotic sarong, she defeats blond, blue-eyed, monied Lois Carson for the title, but only through the intervention of Leonard Rodriguez, who uncovers the teachers and secretaries' plot to stuff the ballot box to avoid having a Japanese queen. The victory infuriates Ko, who criticizes bold American females and insists that Jeanne display traditional Japanese propriety. He arrives at a compromise: Jeanne can be carnival queen if she signs up for *odori* lessons. After ten lessons, the odori teacher rejects her because she smiles too much.

Commentary

The **internal monologue** which Jeanne conducts with herself delineates the complex issues which she carries into adulthood. Philosophically, Jeanne remarks that she feels less discouraged by racist exclusion than by "watching Radine's success." Either refusing to envy Radine or denying envy, Jeanne accepts her Oriental face, which contrasts with the "young, beautifully blond and blue-eyed high school girl moving through a room full of others her own age, much admired by everyone, men and women both, myself included." The experience "empties" Jeanne, short-circuiting her dreams of fulfillment.

Ironically, in victory, Jeanne knows no contentment. Mama, who is sensitive to her youngest's trials, helps with the selection of a dress without actually **identifying** with Jeanne's predicament. The binding force between mother and daughter is love and mutual respect of feminine needs to be admired and accepted. Whereas Ko refuses Jeanne the opportunity to blossom, Mama takes the diplomatic road by accompanying her on a shopping trip and helping her to perceive herself as beautiful in a "frilly ball gown that covered almost everything and buried my legs under layers of ruffles."

The night of the ball is more dismaying than the Wakatsukis realize. Jeanne's decision to wear an ante-bellum gown settles the matter of immodest display, but the voluminous skirts contrast with the more up-to-date styles worn by her maids of honor. The attendants exacerbate Jeanne's isolation by making inane comments about how much they love Chinese food. The music, selected to honor the "girl of my dreams," succeeds in setting Jeanne outside the circle of girls who fulfill Caucasian male fantasies.

As the center of attention, Jeanne treads a bride's gait across a bedsheet carpet to a plywood throne. Mental torment over her *Gone with the Wind* dress destroys the moment and forces the real **issue**

50

"Who had they voted for? Somebody I wanted to be. And wasn't. Who was I then?" Returning to the bewildered Alice-in-Wonderland figure, Jeanne confronts the challenge of adulthood, a stage of life when she can no longer "believe in princesses and queens." Pathless in the stuffy gym, she makes her way through adolescent quandary to the end of a wretched charade.

_____

- **bobbysoxer**   a typical American teen in the 40s.

- **Jean Harlow**   a movie star and platinum blond sex symbol of the 1930s.

Part III

CHAPTER 22

Summary

Opening the final stage of her **memoir** with an original seven-teen-syllable **haiku**, Jeanne indicates that much anguish will precede her acceptance of the past. Unlike Woody, who made the coming-of-age passage in 1946, Jeanne will require another two decades "to accumulate the confidence to deal with what the equivalent experience would have to be for me." Following a partial thawing of frozen feelings in 1966, she and Jim drive their eleven-year-old daughter and five-year-old twin boy and girl to Manzanar in April 1972. The family passes through the Sierras amid Mojave dust and arrives at two gatehouses and other familiar buildings. The Manzanar high school is being used as a city maintenance depot; not much else remains, but Jeanne reconstructs memories from the rocky debris that lies along the camp's fading outlines.

After her family has seen all there is to see and turned toward the car, Jeanne remains alone, eyeing the dark-haired beauty of her eldest child, who is about the age that Jeanne was when Manzanar closed. Able at last to let go of the twenty-five-year phantasm, Jeanne bids farewell to Manzanar, but acknowledges the lingering presence, which "would always live in my nervous system, a needle with Mama's voice." Searching deeper into the tangled, semi-submerged melange of feelings, Jeanne locates a handhold—Papa's defiance, an image that becomes "the rest of my inheritance." In his madcap ranting, he had put value where it belonged—a determination to spend money for a flashy new (even if used) car to avoid the shame of returning like animals in a stinking, crowded bus. He would reclaim his family's freedom in style.

Commentary

Through **first-person narration**, Jeanne communicates intensely personal information in a straightforward, unsentimental style in this final section of the novel. The first of the Wakatsukis to gain a college education and the first to marry a non-Asian, she sets high standards for herself, particularly after the demoralizing three-year detainment in Manzanar. Apparently unencumbered by racist baggage, she gives birth to three mixed-race children and admits to repressing the past by perceiving it as a dream and joking with her siblings about internment. Yet, the experience shared with Kiyo in which an old lady wished that all "dirty Japs" would return to Japan needles Jeanne with an unverbalized hurt.

In a **surrealistic montage**, Jeanne, like Woody in the post-war milieu of Hiroshima, experiences a rush of spiritual contact with those who died and were buried on Manzanar grounds. Although the outlines of the hospital, latrines, and showers are obscured, the typically Japanese rock gardens remain, a tribute to "something enduringly human." She abstracts herself from the experience of walking the once-familiar terrain and views the site from an archeological point of view. Sounds of laughter and the words from the song "Beautiful Dreamer" invoke a sleepwalking state as past merges with present: Jeanne, the ten-year-old schoolgirl, alongside Jeanne, the mother of three. Rich cultural memories coalesce as she recalls the burning of orange peels as an insect repellent and men passing the time in games of *goh* and *hana*.

Symbolic of internees in general and the Wakatsukis in particular, the pear trees, once Ko's personal garden, still survive, "stunted, tenacious, tough, the way a cactus has to be." The **sense impressions** of twisted branches heady with fragrance rhapsodize the scene for Jeanne, in contrast to the realism of her rambunctious children, who "[demand] to know what we were going to *do* out here." Returning to the **persona** of mother, Jeanne agrees that Manzanar, more state of mind than actual place, is "No place for kids."

• **pagoda** an Oriental temple shaped like a tower and topped with a whimsical roof with upturned corners.

- **alluvial fan** clay, sand, gravel, silt, and other debris deposited in a triangle where a stream pours from a gorge.

- *goh* a board game similar to chess.

- *hana* a card game played with Japanese cards which are decorated with *hana*, or flowers, rather than ace, king, queen, jack or spades, hearts, diamonds, and clubs.

- *yogores* ruffians, or hooligans.

CRITICAL ESSAYS

STYLE

Telling her story in **first person**, Jeanne the writer, in collaboration with her husband James, presents an uncluttered reminiscence of World War II. Unlike young Caucasian children of the era, Jeanne the character joins thousands of Japanese-American youngsters in confronting the difficulties of growing up during worldwide hostilities. The **siege mentality** creates a bond among an easily identified non-Caucasian people who suffer silent banishment, far from population centers on the ragged edge of California's wasteland. Out of the range of neighborhood prejudice, they enjoy a safe bondage made bearable by the unity of fellow Japanese Americans. The fact that decades pass before judicial authorities acknowledge the wrong done to a maligned, ostracized racial group indicates how isolated and forgotten the internees were during an era weighted down with fear, sacrifice, insecurity, and loss.

To achieve an unbiased **reportage**, the authors rely on a variety of rhetorical methods: much of the book is simple **chronology**, a month-by-month narration of events, some traumatic, but most—like swing music, baton twirling, and Sears, Roebuck catalogs—idiosyncratic to the children who lived their formative years in the 1940s. Enhancing that time frame is Jeanne's foreword and an introductory **time line**, which sets the **plot** in a historical framework beginning with the first Japanese settlers arriving in Sacramento, California, in 1869 and concluding with Public Law 414 in 1952, an event which granted "Japanese aliens the right to become naturalized U.S. citizens." Abbreviated and abstracted from human emotions, the list of dates and events merely prefaces the struggle of a people to create a home among North American whites.

Two appropriate touches round out the preface: a single **quotation** from a 1947 issue of *Harper's Magazine* decrying the racist motives behind the Japanese relocation program and a gentle **poem** written twenty years later by a member of another oppressed, war-ravaged Oriental nation. The cyclical **motif** of birth and death provides the Houstons a sturdy springboard for a book which carries Jeanne from a child of six to a mother of an eleven-year-old daughter and five-year-old twins. As with most earthly truths, the lessons gained at Manzanar are reasserted to each generation so that, hopefully, subsequent eras will avoid the bigotry of their forebears. Thus Jeanne and Jim Houston familiarize their own children with the place where mother, grandmother and grandfather, Uncle Woody, Aunt Chizu, and Granny spent the war years.

A major factor in the Houstons' success is the skillful inclusion of **details**, such as the boys' formation of a band known as the Jive Bombers, the absurd spectacle of newly outfitted internees in Chaplinesque GI baggy pants, Woody's gift of fifty pounds of sugar to his great Aunt Toyo, Ko's crude wine still, and the relentless sweep of searchlights during riots that erupt at the first anniversary of the bombing of Pearl Harbor. Jeanne's skillful separation of meaningful bits from a heap of memories sets her apart from the average autobiographer. For instance, she assigns Mama a diminished role in the dialogue and action of the book, but one scene robes her in unforgettable strength:

> She reached into the red velvet case, took out a dinner plate and hurled it at the floor right in front of [the dealer's] feet. The man leaped back shouting, "Hey! Hey, don't do that! Those are valuable dishes!" Mama took out another dinner plate and hurled it at the floor, then another and another, never moving, never opening her mouth, just quivering and glaring at the retreating dealer, with tears streaming down her cheeks. . . . When he was gone she stood there smashing cups and bowls and platters until the whole set lay in scattered blue and white fragments across the wooden floor.

Like cups matching saucers, Mama's defiance of exploitation and devaluation befits her grief. The act, appropriate to the **atmosphere** of hurried exodus, suggests that the Wakatsukis have enough self-possession to survive loss as well as to trounce seedy scavengers who circle like sharks.

In contrast to the dramatic dish-smashing scene, some of the most memorable details incorporate **humor**, an essential ingredient in the Wakatsukis' grip on sanity as their world turns upside down and jolts them from a comfortable, secure lifestyle. For example, while searching for identity amid Manzanar's jumble of activities, Jeanne naively follows the mean-spirited advice of Reiko and Mitsue, who advise, "A good dancer must have good skin. . . . In order to have good skin you must rub Rose Brilliantine Hair Tonic in your face and rub cold cream in your hair." Jeanne's compliance captures the humiliation that most children suffer when they are victimized by jeering, unprincipled peers.

As the book draws to a close, the authors return to Ko's harumscarum escapades, which buoy Jeanne "with the first bubbly sense of liberation his defiant craziness had brought along with it. I believed in him completely just then, believed in the fierceness flashing in his wild eyes." She concludes that laughter "would get us past whatever waited inside the fearful dark cloud, get us past the heat and the rattlers, and a great deal more."

Another useful facet of the Houstons' command of nonfiction is **contrast**—scenes of despair or grief or confusion offsetting moments of jubilation, particularly, the birth of a grandchild, Ray's gluttonous grazing among the mess halls, Woody's insistent patriotism, the polite sharing of a modesty shield in the women's toilet, and Papa's drubbing of a political adversary. Such diversions remind the audience that life at Manzanar encompassed the gamut of human emotions, from sadness and self-reproach to shared joys, courtesy, and pride in accomplishment. The key to contrast is the rhythmic pairing of memories, good with bad, fearful with confident, frustration with coping. A strong **image** in the cheerless rows of barracks is Mama, returning from her dietician's job, topped with a "bright yellow, longbilled sun hat she had made herself and always kept stiffly starched." Against the rigidity of camp routine, Mama's personal standards are even starchier as the bonnet, engulfed in heat waves, and becomes "a yellow flower wavering in the glare."

Tidbits of **historical analysis** dot the text, as with the comparison of Japanese freedom to that of emancipated black slaves:

> In the government's eyes a free man now, [Ko] sat, like those black slaves you hear about who, when they got word of their freedom at the end of the Civil War, just did not know

where else to go or what else to do and ended up back on the plantation, rooted there out of habit or lethargy or fear.

A second example contrasts the internees with "an Indian who turned up one Saturday billing himself as a Sioux chief, wearing bear claws and head feathers." His dance, appropriate to time and place, meets with the internees' approval as they identify with Caucasian attempts at racial cleansing of Native Americans, which lasted three centuries in contrast to the internees' three years. These philosophical comments set the Japanese experience in context with every citizen's experience with democracy, whether Irish American, African American, Asian American, or Native American. Well placed segments of **dialogue** provide the reader a snatch of conversation among internees—for example, the exchange between Jeanne's parents:

Mama said, "Ko."
No answer.
"Ko?"
"What?"
"What are we going to do?"
"Wait."
"For what?" she asked.
"Listen to me. I have an idea."

The **rhythms** of exchange between Jeanne's parents delineate the style of everyday communication, which, against a backdrop of camp tension, can explode into harsh words, suspicions, drunken singing of the Japanese national anthem, or childish ranting and **sloganeering.** Yet, the release provided by incendiary or emotional words supplants the need to use fists, guns, or sabotage to combat unlawful incarceration. Like the valve on a steam engine, language is an important outlet to pent-up hostilities.

Occasional touches of **lyricism** remind the reader that poetry springs from the humblest and most unlikely settings—for example, Jeanne's perception that

It is so characteristically Japanese, the way lives were made more tolerable by gathering loose desert stones and forming with them something enduringly human. These rock gardens had outlived the barracks and the towers and would surely outlive the asphalt road and rusted pipes and shat-

56

tered slabs of concrete. Each stone was a mouth, speaking for a family, for some man who had beautified his doorstep.

Such **metaphoric** witnesses to will symbolize a universal truth about human endurance—as the adage advises, they turn lemons into lemonade by evolving methods of enduring out of the simplest media. To pass idle time and ease frustrations, Ko and other heads of household arrange stones into patterned walks as though paving from bedrock a handmade path to a new life. In this assertion of creativity lies hope that Manzanar is a brief stop along a greater, more significant passage.

SETTINGS

The harsh, unfriendly **location** of Manzanar parallels the brutality of confinement. Contrasting with their Long Beach home, where the Wakatsukis scooped up grunion on a moonlit beach, ate at a communal table, and watched the departing *Nereid* from the neighborhood wharf, Jeanne reconstructs the tight configuration of rows of barracks, latrines, school, and hospital, the overseeing guardhouses, the chlorine shed, and the shadow of MPs, never far away from ordinary activities such as hopscotch, reading, and gazing out over the Mojave. Much of the physical discomfort of internment comes from nature itself—the whirling dust storms which pierce cubicle walls, the craggy face of Mount Whitney, and the extremes of heat and cold, for which the families are inadequately prepared.

Jeanne relieves gritty, depressing scenes with glimpses of her family in other locales. Woody, assigned to duty in post-war Japan, visits the memorial tombstone dedicated to Ko in 1913. Ushered into his Aunt Toyo's residence, he observes

an immaculate rock garden, its sand white and freshly raked. A hedge of high bamboo ordered it. Inside, the rooms were almost empty—a large, once elegant country house stripped of all but a few mats, an altar in one corner of the first room, a funeral urn. They had not been hit by bombs. The war itself, the years of losing, had turned the house into a clean, swept, airy skeleton.

In her own disjointed post-war resettlement, Jeanne is driven from

Manzanar to Long Beach, with its "palm-lined boulevards, past the busy rows of shops and markets, the lawns and driveways of quiet residential streets." To a returning refugee, the six-hour drive is "a time machine, as if, in March of 1942 one had lifted his foot to take a step, had set it down in October of 1945, and was expected just to keep on walking, with all intervening time erased." Additional bits of locale take brothers and sisters east to New Jersey, Mama back to the fish cannery, Ko to his home studio and drawing board, and Jeanne to high school. After the family moves a second time, to a strawberry farm in Santa Clara, she indicates her disinterest in farming and her absorption in teen concerns by giving no details of home. The most vivid scene is her elongated processional down the bed-sheeted royal way to "its plywood finale"—a throne honoring a carnival queen who is ridiculed by several of her resentful female attendants.

Part 3, the most intense description of place, brings Jeanne full circle to the site now synonymous with Japanese-American oppression—Manzanar, which was actually one of ten internment camps. Like a conductor calling out stops, she mentally records the miles from Santa Cruz down Route 101 to Paso Robles, from the Diablo Range around Bakersfield, through Tehachapi Pass and on to the Mojave. The tension in her voice resonates the last miles, beyond "two oases, the first at Olancha, the second around Lone Pine, a small, tree-filled town" and on to a scene dominated by "sagebrush, tumbleweeds, and wind." The sketchy remains of what used to be a fair-sized, ready-made city poke up from the sand like remnants of a ghost town: a pillbox, elms, cattle guard, white obelisk memorializing the dead, spigot, and flagpole circle. The scent of spring blossoms and the single stepping stone that once served as someone's front stoop bring back homier memories of a time when Ko and Mama sat on the steps deciding how to make the long trek back to civilized life. The zany vision of Ko steering his car on a shredded front tire replays Ko's indomitable spirit as he yells to onlookers his jubilant **rhyme**, "No bus for us! No bus for us!"

THEMES

Growing out of a crucial test of American democracy and world order, *Farewell to Manzanar* functions on several levels:

As a **slice of history**, the book epitomizes the status of civil rights as viewed by people who lose freedoms from 1941 to 1945 for the sake of national security. Working from **nonfiction** data, Jeanne and James Houston recreate non-judgmental pictures of California citizens terrorized by an enemy attack on the Hawaiian islands. Knowing that the West Coast could be the next target, local people raise no cry against FBI agents who arrest likely collaborators, particularly Jeanne's father, whose job takes him by private boat beyond the coast, where he could easily contact the Japanese military and pass on fuel or information about Terminal Island, a spit of land shared by Japanese-American residents and the U.S. Navy.

A serious theme imbedded in the furor and insecurity resulting from the bombing of Pearl Harbor consists of three questions:

- Who has rights?
- What must the government do to protect those rights?
- What must the government do to prevent the Asian-American segment of the population from violating U.S. loyalties in order to satisfy loyalty to the Old Country?

A vast number of internees have relatives and ties with Japan. Some Japanese Americans were educated in Japan, preserve traditions and customs, honor Shinto and Buddhist rites, correspond and visit with citizens of Japan, and speak and write the Japanese language. Executive Order 9066 implies that those ties and traditions to the former homeland must remain dormant and non-threatening until all danger of attack has passed and the U.S. is once more free of menace by Japanese bombs.

President Roosevelt's quick action on matters of national security seem, on the surface, to represent the **common good**, which is an essential aspect of his role as commander in chief of the military. However, Japanese Americans were interned under severe scrutiny—compared to the treatment of Italian Americans and German Americans, who also maintained Old Country ties with enemy nations. No less a threat than potential Japanese saboteurs, people with links to Germany and Italy received no harassment or inquisition equivalent to that suffered by people of Japanese ancestry. The obvious conclusion is that, unlike European Americans, Japanese Americans are **racially identifiable**. Because their physical features reflected the hated Tojo, fanatical kamikaze, and the Emperor of Japan, Caucasian hysteria viewed Japanese Americans as a highly visible—and hateable—target.

When the war ended, Italian Americans and German Americans faced no great loss of home, possessions, income, or reputation. They returned to the mainstream of Caucasian America. Japanese Americans, who were released 1,000 at a time from internment camps, crept back into freedom as veritable paupers, whipped in spirit and pocketbook. Their sons, many of whom returned from the war scarred by the experience or encased in coffins, received no accolades for unusually demanding service. Not only did former internees grieve for their children, the lost years, interrupted lives, and the humiliation of American-style concentration camps, but they also bore the burden of America's use of atomic force against Hiroshima and Nagasaki, two civilian cities where friends and relatives died cataclysmic deaths or survived under the threat of future cancers engendered by radiation.

As a depiction of **coming of age**, *Farewell to Manzanar* records one girl's efforts to reach womanhood with a strong sense of self. Against the backdrop of incarceration, separation from father and, later, brothers and sisters, and enrollment in a school where the teacher pointedly ignores her, Jeanne experiences the usual insecurities and challenges that mold young children into sturdy adults. **Resilience** and **self-sufficiency**, both major factors in her success, inspire numerous methods of passing time, coping with deprivation, and learning to live in crowded conditions with a severely dysfunctional family.

An integral part of coming of age is **rebellion**, an attitude which Jeanne shares with brothers Kiyo and Woody and father, Ko. No less insistent on individuality than the others, Jeanne reaches out to neighborhood children who also live on the periphery of social acceptance—Hispanics who teach her native songs and a lower-class white boy from North Carolina, who kisses as though he means it. Hungering for attention, Jeanne joins the motley array of Cabrillo Homes teenagers and copes well with diversity.

Like Ko, Jeanne's perception of marriage diverges from the accepted pattern. Her role models reveal incremental steps toward assimilation. Granny, who speaks no English, treasures Japanese valuables. Ko, the Wakatsuki black sheep, prefers autonomy in a land of promise to diminished status in Japan, where his father fell short of the Samurai status of Ko's grandfather. Working the American dream to his benefit, Ko garners numerous skills—fishing, farming, denture and furniture making, orchard pruning, and translation. Mama, who was intended as the bride of a farmer, exacerbates his autocratic streak by eloping with him and raising children remarkably similar to their parents in individuality.

Jeanne, no less a challenge to Ko's authority than Woody or Kiyo, cultivates friendship with Radine, the stereotypical blond, flirtatious all-American miss who flourished in the 1940s. Content with Asian features, Jeanne comments, "I never wanted to change my face or to be someone other than myself. What I wanted was the kind of acceptance that seemed to come so easily to Radine." The only route to an acceptable level of social acceptance was through defiance of Ko and emulation of Radine.

As a glimpse of **family**, the story depicts a universal truth—that children often adopt their parents' idiosyncracies by applying them to new situations. For Jeanne and Woody, the future does not lie in physical emigration from Japan but in spiritual emigration from tradition. The tensions brought about by arguments, Ko's ultimatums, and an undercurrent of misbehavior and challenge push Woody into tedious arguments and Jeanne to the extremes of her love-hate relationship with Ko.

The sufferings of Manzanar are summed up in Jeanne's wavering regard for her father. She visualizes her shame at Manzanar in terms of Ko's downfall. She admires his pluck; she abhors his vulgarity and bluster. When Mama takes over the family's financial support, Jeanne confesses that Papa no longer deserves respect, an admission which wounds her more deeply than it hurts Ko. The aspects of Ko's personality which fill her with pride are the qualities she pursues. Yet, it is impossible for her, a modern American female, to emulate Oriental male bravado. Her struggle leads her far afield to the formation of a new nuclear unit, the first Wakatsuki to marry out of her race and produce mixed-race children.

As an exposition of **Japanese tradition**, the narrative does justice to its opening premise, that Issei, Nisei, and Sansei share no single point of view. Forced to state their loyalties with a *yes, yes or no,* or *no* on two oaths, the mixed generations reach critical mass. Woody, the conciliatory brother who gets what he wants through compromise, takes a job as carpenter and awaits the draft rather than volunteer for induction into the army. To him, the question of loyalty to Old Country or to the U.S. lies in action: "The more of us who go into the army, the sooner the war will be over, the sooner you and Mama will be out of here."

Peacetime issues such as the nuts and bolts of everyday living delineate the Japanese urge for **unity** and **harmony**. In crowded latrines, women offer each other the courtesy of a pasteboard modesty shield and bow politely to express a mutual distaste for the distressing situation, to which they refuse to surrender their civility. Likewise, mealtimes herd families through chow lines in barbaric assembly-line fashion, but Japanese tradition restores the niceties of home through shared pots of tea and whatever amenities can be squeezed out of small gardens, visits, and the singing of the Japanese national anthem.

Amply sprinkled with Japanese equivalents for *flower, stupid, hoodlums, massage, stoic philosophy, traditional dance, traditional theater, woven mats,* and the lyrics to the Japanese national anthem, the text draws the reader into a foreign culture by providing **context clues**, such as the peripheral description of Jeanne's efforts to *momo* (massage) Mama's back by loosening tense muscles with therapeutic pokes and jabs. The Houstons downplay foreignness by emphasizing the aspects of living that returnees share with other racial groups and social levels at Cabrillo Homes. By maintaining **control** of such details, the authors focus on the themes of freedom, rights, and sacrifice, which preoccupied the entire nation until V-J Day.

ASIAN AMERICANS AND THE LAW

Partly as a result of expansion and the Gold Rush of 1849, West Coast industry stepped up the importation of Chinese and Japanese laborers in the nineteenth century. Unfortunately, these foreigners were often ill-treated and ill-fed by their employers, and many of them died from work-related injuries and illnesses to which they had no natural immunity. Those who survived became an important ingredient in the building of the first intercontinental railroad, as well as in mining, agriculture, canneries, logging, fishing, meatpacking, and salt production. Asian workers quickly earned a reputation as steady, efficient, dependable workers. These qualities, however, worked to their disadvantage by bringing them into competition with whites, who soon pressed for laws granting citizenship to only whites and nonwhites of African descent. Thus, California's Alien Land Act of 1913 declared Asian Americans ineligible not only for citizenship but also for property ownership. A 1920 law prevented anyone who owned land from selling it to Asians or leaving it to Asian heirs. To circumvent outright disenfranchisement, Asian-born entrepreneurs deeded new purchases to the Nissei, their American-born offspring, or Kibei, Japanese Americans who were educated in Japan.

Urban Japanese often found successful careers in food service, laundries and tailor shops, domestic employ, gardening, shopkeeping, hotel service, bathhouses, and barber shops. To strengthen their financial base, family-run businesses networked with other Asian-American suppliers, laborers, and small loan companies. Such community-based connectedness became the lifeline of immigrants who found large, white-owned banks closed to their needs. To assure a stable population, Issei, or native-born Japanese, sought Japanese brides, some by mail order from Japan and others from Hawaii. They developed their own law enforcement, insurance, fraternal, burial, and educational associations, as well as their own worship centers. Thus a sense of unity strengthened and enlarged a closed community which rapidly rivaled the less cohesive white population.

By 1920, even more laws began to encroach on Japanese-American success. California legislation prohibited Japanese employers from hiring white females and charged prohibitively high rates for fishing licenses. Authorities stated outright the purpose of such measures: to limit privileges for immigrant Japanese so that fewer nationals would leave Japan to seek opportunity in the United States.

These West Coast restrictions did not go unnoticed in Washington. President Theodore Roosevelt, as a gesture to Japan, ordered an end to segregated schools. The Japanese government reciprocated by limiting the number of nationals who were allowed to emigrate.

By 1924, pressures from voters forced Congress to establish a quota system as a means of stabilizing living and working conditions in California, Oregon, and Washington—states in which Asian immigrants often outnumbered established racial groups—that is, whites, Indians, and Hispanics. The force which finally broke the prejudicial laws was the growth of the second wave of Asian Americans, the Nissei, or those born in the United States and endowed with constitutional protections to property, education, land ownership, voting, and office-holding rights.

To solidify anti-Asian forces, whites began to form leagues, labor unions, and clubs such as the American Legion and the Native Sons and Daughters of the Golden West, all of which excluded Japanese Americans. To counter with their own unifying organization, the newcomers formed the powerful Japanese-American Citizens League, which reached national status by 1930.

Following the traumatic uprooting of Japanese immigrants and Japanese Americans during the WWII years, continued upheaval weakened resolve among many of those who suffered the most— particularly the loss of health, livelihood, homes, and personal property. Many fled the West Coast, where blatant anti-Asian slogans prohibited them from seeking jobs and housing. However, by 1950, Japanese Americans began to return west to compete with a growing mix of southern blacks, Mexican Hispanics, and local whites.

In 1952, under the direction of the Supreme Court, the old order of restrictive laws and prejudicial treatment ended with a repeal of the Alien Land Act of 1913. Japanese Americans began to invest directly in their nation through business, public office, and integrated neighborhoods. That same year, Congress passed Public Law 414, granting Japanese aliens the right to become naturalized citizens of the United States.

EXECUTIVE ORDER 9066

The paperwork which set this story in motion is a barely comprehensible, bureaucratic five-paragraph order signed by Franklin D. Roosevelt at the White House on February 19, 1942. Overall, the wording reiterates a constitutional fact—that the U.S. President functions as commander in chief of the military and exerts ultimate power during dangerous times. The document reads:

> Whereas the successful prosecution of the war requires every possible protection against espionage and against sabotage to national-defense material, national-defense premises, and national-defense utilities as defined in Section 4, Act of April 20, 1918, 40 Stat. 533, as amended by the Act of November 30, 1940, 54 Stat. 1220, and the Act of August 21, 1941, 55 Stat. 655 (U.S.C., Title 50, Sec. 104), now, therefore, by virtue of the authority vested in me as President of the United States, and Commander in Chief of the Army and Navy, I hereby authorize and direct the Secretary of

War, and the Military Commanders whom he may from time to time designate, whenever he or any designated Commander deems such action necessary or desirable, to prescribe military areas in such places and of such extent as he or the appropriate Military Commander may determine, from which any or all persons may be excluded, and with respect to which, the right of any person to enter, remain in, or leave shall be subject to whatever restrictions the Secretary of War or the appropriate Military Commander may impose in his discretion. The Secretary of War is hereby authorized to provide for residents of any such area who are excluded therefrom, such transportation, food, shelter, and other accommodations as may be necessary, in the judgment of the Secretary of War or the said Military Commander, and until other arrangements are made, to accomplish the purpose of this order. The designation of military areas in any region or locality shall supersede designations of prohibited and restricted areas by the Attorney General under the Proclamations of December 7 and 8, 1941, and shall supersede the responsibility and authority of the Attorney General under the said Proclamations in respect of such prohibited and restricted areas.

I hereby further authorize and direct the Secretary of War and the said Military Commanders to take such other steps as he or the appropriate Military Commander may deem advisable to enforce compliance with the restrictions applicable to each Military area hereinabove authorized to be designated, including the use of Federal troops and other Federal Agencies, with authority to accept assistance of state and local agencies.

I hereby further authorize and direct all executive Departments, independent establishments and other Federal Agencies, to assist the Secretary of War or the said Military Commanders in carrying out this Executive Order including the furnishing of medical aid, hospitalization, food, clothing, transportation, use of land, shelter, and other supplies, equipment, utilities, facilities, and services.

This order shall not be construed as modifying or limiting in any way the authority heretofore granted under Executive Order No. 8972, dated December 12, 1941, nor shall it be construed as limiting or modifying the duty and responsibility of the Federal Bureau of Investigation, with respect to the investigation of alleged acts of sabotage or the duty and responsibility of the Attorney General and the Department of Justice under the Proclamations of December 7 and 8, 1941, prescribing regulations for the conduct and control of alien enemies, except as such duty and responsibility is superseded by the designation of military areas hereunder.

[**Note:** At no time do the words *Japanese Americans*, *internment*, or *civil rights* appear in the document, nor does the order appear to be aimed at one racial group.]

CHARACTER ANALYSES

The contrast of characters is the life's blood of *Farewell to Manzanar*, the fulcrum on which the authors place their weight to lift the memoir into the reader's field of vision. Most significant to the text are Jeanne, the youngest of ten children, and her parents.

JEANNE WAKATSUKI HOUSTON

Jeanne, who successfully forces herself back to a childlike state, recounts hopes, aspirations, responsibilities, and disappointments from the point of view of her earlier self. Along the way to adulthood, she stumbles over more adversity than the average American child ever encounters. Manzanar becomes the unfair burden thrust on Jeanne's back by two nations at war. She remains flexible and resilient; her methods of escape reflect an ability to improvise. If Papa won't allow conversion to Catholicism, then dance lessons may be even better. If prayer won't produce apricots from the Almighty, maybe she should read more books and plunge deeper into the fantasy world of princesses and queens. Like Rapunzel letting down her hair, Jeanne uncoils the traditions that bind Japanese women to a rigid patriarchy. Her too-wide smile, which defeats a geisha and an *odori* instructor and infuriates her old-school father, defines the face of the all-American girl. More attuned to the sweater-clad World War II Betty Grables than mincing Japanese beauties or dramatic kabuki dancers, Jeanne picks her costume—a braided majorette outfit, baton, and white boots. The getup lands her one firm Caucasian female friend and a host of admiring males. For Jeanne, the lesson makes sense—give them what they want, but keep your distance.

The arrival of puberty puts Jeanne in a quandary—whether to fake a traditional Japanese femininity or compete for carnival queen. Her choice produces a **paradox**, the stereotypical bitter-sweet taste of an unfulfilling victory, which shoves her face-to-face with bigotry in the form of girls who patronize her Oriental heritage while planning a post-coronation party which does not include her. Jeanne omits the ensuing years which acclimate her to the Caucasian world and assure her that marriage to an Anglo and mother-hood of Anglo-Japanese children are right and proper.

KO WAKATSUKI

Most significant to Jeanne's survival of internment is her sur-vival of her father's manic-depressive antics. In the early days, when she shares Mama's bed and wears baggy World War I surplus garb, her giggles bubble happily to the surface. Ko's return, how-ever, tips the delicate balance of a family on the edge. His alcohol-ism and unbridled outbursts terrify Jeanne, who has no easy access to escape. Like the contrasting **masks of the theater**, Ko, the dual enemy/savior of the Wakatsuki family, struts with pride, but batters against a wall of local accusation that he has gained release from Fort Lincoln through collaboration.

Boldly rejecting the label of *inu* and thrusting himself out of self-imposed house arrest, Ko turns his cane into a swagger stick, a mark of pride in manhood. Capable of cowing Woody into postpon-ing military service until a draft notice makes it obligatory, Ko climbs back to the managerial spot in the Wakatsuki household and a position of importance as reader and translator of the newspaper to inmates who can't read English. While Mama works at the hospi-tal, he retires from work and devotes himself to simple pleasures, puttering about his rock garden, making dentures, and building furniture.

The real test of Ko's resilience is his proferred freedom, which he rejects until government edicts force him to return to civilian life. Because he has acclimated himself to West Coast life, he rejects the call of his children to New Jersey and drives his family home to

Long Beach via three round trips across the desert. At Cabrillo Homes, he continues spinning dreams of success through a Japanese-built housing project and a failed venture into the dried abalone business. At length he acknowledges that he must return to farming.

In Santa Clara, Ko fades from the picture. Jeanne indicates that he breaks his self-destructive addiction to alcohol and succeeds at strawberry growing. His insistence that his tenth child follow Japanese codes of conduct reveals that he has no intention of loosening his grip on the role of **paterfamilias**. For Jeanne, the worst of Ko's headstrong individuality is his appearance at a PTA honors ceremony, where he humiliates her with an overly formalized obeisance inappropriate to the situation.

MAMA WAKATSUKI

Perhaps the key to understanding both Jeanne and Ko is Mama, the quiet, unselfish matriarch who never quails at Ko's extravagances and who follows pragmatism as surely as Columbus set his course by the North Star. When money is needed, she locates work in the West Coast fish canneries and as a dietician at Manzanar. When family comfort is threatened, she mobilizes her crew in padding the barracks to keep out dust. When Jeanne needs guidance in how to look like a well-brought-up young lady, Mama superintends the shopping trip which locates the poufy dress which will showcase her daughter's beauty without sacrificing modesty. For whatever **yin** that arises, Mama provides the **yang**.

Toward Ko, Mama maintains a **passive aggressive** stance. She is able to conciliate, smooth over, or ignore detrimental behaviors which endanger family harmony, such as Ko's refusal to eat in the mess hall or his menacing of Mama's aged mother. When he plunges to the bottom of despair and threatens to kill Mama, she simply waits for him to finish the act. Outfoxed by Mama's refusal to share in his maudlin **melodrama**, Ko respects her, yet distances himself from her strength. While his resources sag at Cabrillo Homes, Mama applies herself more energetically to physical labor. In typical Asian style, she bears the burdens without complaint, grows stronger, and outlives her flamboyant husband. Overall, Jeanne owes much of her indomitable courage and foresight to both parents. A blend of Papa's stubborn **exhibitionism** and Mama's altruistic care for the people around her, Jeanne has her way and marries out of her race. Following years of motherhood, Jeanne at last puts herself first and leads her family to the source of a vexatious nettle that must be excised in order for her to know peace. In the guise of the **objective** archeologist, she locates shards of the past on the windswept grounds of Manzanar. Rapidly, her objectivity fades into memories of home.

Playing through Jeanne's mind are the videotapes which all children recall in times of stress. When adulthood weighs heavier than the spirit can bear, the mind shucks off maturity. Disengaged from the grown-up Jeanne, like Alice-down-the-rabbit-hole, she returns to Papa's lap, Woody's big-brother protection, and Mama's **homilies**. The disembodied voices that Jeanne absorbs from Manzanar are not those of ghosts. They emerge intact from past scenes, long suppressed, of a defiant dad too proud to ride the bus back to Long Beach. They emerge from Mama, the selfless dietician who nurtures others with the spiritual food that will make them strong.

REVIEW QUESTIONS AND ESSAY TOPICS

(1) Compare the speaker's wartime deprivations and confinement with those depicted in *The Diary of Anne Frank*, Ernst Schnabel's *Anne Frank: A Portrait in Courage*, Corrie ten Boom's *The Hiding Place*, Esther Hautzig's *The Endless Steppe*, Kurt Vonnegut's *Slaughterhouse-Five*, Max Garcia's *As Long As I Remain Alive*, Everett Alvarez, Jr.'s *Chained Eagle*, and Elie Wiesel's *Night*. Enumerate characteristics which enable victims to remain alive and later recover from trauma.

(2) Compare the speaker's response to racial prejudice with that of the speakers in Maya Angelou's *I Know Why the Caged Bird Sings*, Bernard Malamud's *The Fixer*, Scott Momaday's *The Way to Rainy Mountain*, Chinua Achebe's *Things Fall Apart*, Alan Paton's *Cry, the Beloved Country*, Theodora Kroeber's *Ishi*, Toni Morrison's *Beloved*, and Yoko Watkins' *So Far From the Bamboo Grove*.

(3) Discuss whether the speaker approaches her wartime experience from the point of view of adulthood or childhood memories. Explain why she departs from first-person point of view to

include the memories of other internees, particularly Kaz at the chlorine shed, Ko at Fort Lincoln, and Woody in Ka-ke.

(4) Account for the time span between Jeanne Houston's departure from Manzanar and her return to confront old ghosts and sad memories. Reconcile her years of silence with current studies of trauma syndrome. Why does the author compare herself to rape victims?

(5) Using *Farewell to Manzanar* as a model, compose extended definitions of memoir, autobiography, haiku, dialogue, Electra complex, saga, and *bildungsroman*.

(6) Compare the speaker's anti-war sentiments with those of Francis FitzGerald's *Fire in the Lake,* Dee Brown's *Bury My Heart at Wounded Knee* or *Creek Mary's Blood,* Joseph Heller's *Catch-22,* Eric Remarque's *All Quiet on the Western Front,* John Hersey's *Hiroshima,* Galt MacDermott, Gerome Ragni, and James Rado's *Hair,* or Dalton Trumbo's *Johnny Got His Gun.*

(7) Create a background study of refugees in literature as found in Pearl Buck's *The Good Earth,* Maxine Hong Kingston's *Woman Warrior,* John Hersey's *Hiroshima,* Kurt Vonnegut's "D.P.," Chung Hua-min and Arthur C. Miller's *Madame Mao,* and James and Jeanne Wakatsuki Houston's *Farewell to Manzanar.*

(8) Compare the speaker's depiction of wartime upheaval with similar themes in films such as *Plenty, Sayonara, From Here to Eternity, Shining Through,* and *Stalag 17.* Emphasize the emotional and spiritual accommodations to trauma which enable people to survive.

(9) Analyze President Franklin Roosevelt's Order 9066, which caused the illegal detention of Asian-Americans. What historical and political pressures forced his decision to confine citizens without compensating them for their losses? What subsequent revelations caused the government to rescind the order?

(10) Read the war poems that evolved from World War II, particularly Randall Jarrell's "Death of the Ball Turret Gunner" and

Yevgeny Yevtushenko's "Baba Yar." Contrast these poets' atti-
tudes to those of Jeanne, her parents and grandparents, and her
siblings, especially Woody.

(11) Contrast the wording of the Bill of Rights with the strictures
of Executive Order 9066. Determine whether President
Roosevelt's decision to intern Japanese Americans was legal
and warranted. Make a similar comparison of Executive Order
9066 with the Emancipation Proclamation.

(12) Jeanne quotes her mother as saying, "Nurture your children
and your family with love and emotional support. Accept
change if it means protecting your loved ones." Apply this philosophy to the task of surviving internment.

(13) Apply Ko's philosophy to Japanese-American cohesiveness:
"Race must not be pitted against race. We do not raise ourselves
at the expense of others. Through co-operation we advance
together as human beings."

(14) Suggest alterations in the Houstons' working method, style,
and tone. For example, explore a multiple point of view
through the words of other family members, teachers, guards,
and civil defense authorities.

(15) Comment on President Franklin Roosevelt's speech delivered
December 8, 1941, in which he said, " . . . we will not only
defend ourselves to the uttermost but will make it very certain
that this form of treachery shall never again endanger us. Hostilities exist. There is no blinking at the fact that our people, our
territory and our interests are in grave danger."

(16) Discuss why Jeanne is more suited to ballet and baton twirling
than to the *odori* dance that arose from traditional Japanese
kabuki drama.

(17) Contrast the focus of the Japanese national anthem with
"Le Marseillaise," "Deutschland Über Alles," "God Save the
Queen," and "The Star-Spangled Banner." What does the theme
of endurance say about Japanese nationalism?

SELECTED BIBLIOGRAPHY

PUBLISHED WORKS

Jeanne Wakatsuki Houston

Memoir

Farewell to Manzanar (with James, 1973)

Screenplays

Farewell to Manzanar (with James Houston and John Korty, 1976)
Barrio (with James Houston, 1978)
The Melting Pot (with James Houston, 1980)

Nonfiction

Don't Cry, It's Only Thunder (with Paul G. Hensler, 1984)
Beyond Manzanar and Other Views of Asian-American Womanhood (1985)

Articles

"Other Days of Infamy" (with James Houston in *Mother Jones*, February/March 1976)
"After the War" in *A Gathering of Flowers: Stories About Being Young in America* (1990)
"Colors," *New England Review*, Spring 1993
"Rock Garden," *Dreamers and Desperadoes* (May 1993) and *Sounds of Writing* (Fall 1993) and also articles in *Ethnic American Woman, Asian Americans: Social and Psychological Perspectives, Ethnic Lifestyles and Mental Health, Common Ground, Crossing Cultures, American Mosaic*, and the *Borzoi College Reader*

James D. Houston

Novels

Between Battles (1968)
Gig (1969)
A Native Son of the Golden West (1971)

Continental Drift (1978)
Love Life (1985)

Short Stories

The Adventures of Charlie Bates (1973)
West Coast Fiction: Modern Writing from California, Oregon and Washington (1979)
Gasoline: The Automotive Adventures of Charlie Bates (1980)

Screenplays

Li'a: The Legacy of a Hawaiian Man (1988)
Listen to the Forest (1991)

Nonfiction

Open Field (with John R. Brodie, 1974)
Three Songs for My Father (1974)
Californians: Searching for the Golden State (1982)
One Can Think About Life After the Fish Is in the Canoe and Other Coastal Stories (1985)

Sketches (1985)

The Men in My Life, and Other More or Less True Recollections of Kinship (1987)

Textbooks

Writing from the Inside (1973)

Editing

California Heartland: Writings from the Great Central Valley (1978)

CRITICAL ANALYSIS

"Adult Books for Young Adults," *Library Journal.* January 15, 1974, 67.

"American Portrait" (video). New York: CBS, Inc., February 13, 1986.

ANDERSON, KATHERINE. "Review of *Farewell to Manzanar,*" *Library Journal,* January 15, 1974, 227.

Book Review Digest, 1974, 576.

BRYANT, DOROTHY. "The School Yearbook with the Barbed-Wire Design," *The Nation,* November 9, 1974, 469.

CRIST, JUDITH. "Review of *Farewell to Manzanar,*" a made-for-TV movie, *TV Guide,* March 5, 1976, A–10.

Contemporary Authors Autobiography Series, Vol. 16. Detroit: Gale Research, 1993.

Contemporary Authors, New Revision Series, Vol. 29. Detroit: Gale Research, 1992.

DONOVAN, JENNIFER. "The Real-Life 'Wonder Women' of 1984," *San Francisco Chronicle,* November 14, 1984, 42.

FRIEDSON, ANTHONY. "No More Farewells: An Interview with Jeanne and James Houston," *Biography,* University of Hawaii Press, Winter, 1984, 50–73.

HOFFMAN, MARILYN. "Moving Beyond Manzanar," *Christian Science Monitor,* January 28, 1985, 25–26.

HOLT, PATRICIA. "James D. Houston," *Publishers Weekly,* September 4, 1978.

KINNELL, S. K., ed. *People in History.* 2 vols. Santa Barbara, California: ABC-Clio, 1988.

LA VIOLETTE, F. E. "Review of *Farewell to Manzanar,*" *Pacific Affairs,* Fall 1974, 405.

MITCHELL, HENRY. "Arriving at a Good-Bye," *Washington Post,* March 5, 1976, B1, B3.

RABINOWITZ, DOROTHY. "Review of *Farewell to Manzanar,*" *Saturday Review,* November 6, 1973, 34.

"Review of *Farewell to Manzanar*," *Book List*, December 15, 1975, 563.

"Review of *Farewell to Manzanar*," *New Yorker*, November 5, 1973, 87–88.

"Review of *Farewell to Manzanar*," *New York Times Book Review*, January 13, 1974, 31.

ROGERS, MICHAEL. "Review of *Farewell to Manzanar*," *Rolling Stone*, December 6, 1973.

SCHICKEL, RICHARD. "Review of teleplay 'Farewell to Manzanar,'" *Time*, March 15, 1976.

TALCOTT, REP. BURT. *Congressional Record*, March 17, 1976, H2033.

WATERS, HARRY. "Review of *Farewell to Manzanar*," a made-for-TV movie, *Newsweek*, March 15, 1976, 55.

WITTY, SUSAN. "An All-American Girl," *Woman's World*, June 18, 1985, 44–45.

HISTORICAL ANALYSIS

BAKER, LILLIAN. *Redress and Reparations Demands by Japanese-Americans*. Medford, Oregon: Webb Research, 1991.

BOSWORTH, ALLAN R. *America's Concentration Camps*. New York: Norton, 1967.

COHEN, ELIE. *Human Behavior in the Concentration Camp*. Westport, Connecticut: Greenwood, 1984.

COLLINS, DONALD E. *Native American Aliens: Disloyalty and the Renunciation of Citizenship by Japanese Americans During World War II*. New York: Greenwood, 1985.

DANIELS, ROGER. *The Decision to Relocate the Japanese Americans.* Melbourne, Florida: Krieger, 1986.

_____, et al., eds. *Japanese Americans, from Relocation to Redress.* Ann Arbor, Michigan: Books Demand UMI, 1991.

DE GRAAF, JOHN. "A Personal Matter: Gordon Hirabayashi vs. the United States" (video). The Constitution Project. San Francisco, California: National Asian American Telecommunications Association, 1992.

DING, LONI. "The Color of Honor" (video). San Francisco, California: National Asian American Telecommunications Association, 1992.

EMBREY, SUE KUNITOMI, et al., eds. *Manzanar Martyr: An Interview with Harry Y. Ueno.* Fullerton, California: CSUF Oral History, 1986.

GEE, DEBORAH. "Slaying the Dragon" (video). CrossCurrent Media. San Francisco, California: National Asian American Telecommunications Association.

GESENSWAY, DEBORAH, and MINDY ROSEMAN. *Beyond Words: Images from America's Concentration Camps.* Ithaca, New York: Cornell University Press, 1987.

HUMANAKA, SHEILA. *The Journey: Japanese Americans, Racism and Renewal.* New York: Orchard Books, 1990.

"Japanese Relocation" (video). Washington, D. C.: University of Washington Instructional Media Services, 1942.

KNAEFLER, TOMI K. *Our House Divided: Seven Japanese American Families in World War Two.* Honolulu, Hawaii: University of Hawaii Press, 1991.

MASUMOTO, DAVID MAS. "Chance to Right a 50-Year-Old Wrong," *USA Today,* August 10, 1992, A3.

MYER, DILLON. *Uprooted Americans: The Japanese Americans and the War Relocation Authority During World War II.* Tucson: University of Arizona Press, 1971.

NAKAMURA, ROBERT A. "Conversations: Before the War/After the War" (video), San Francisco, California: National Asian American Telecommunications Association, 1992.

_____. "Manzanar" (video) Visual Communications. San Francisco, California: National Asian American Telecommunications Association, 1971.

"Personal Justice Denied." Washington, D.C.: U.S. Government Printing Office, 1983.

SONE, MONICA. *Nisei Daughter.* Seattle, Washington: University of Washington Press, 1979.

TAJIRI, VINCENT, ed. *Through Innocent Eyes: Teen-agers' Impressions of World War II Internment Camp Life.* Keiro Services, 1990.

WEGLYN, MICHI. *Years of Infamy: The Untold Story of America's Concentration Camps.* New York: Morrow, 1978.

YOSHIDA, MICHAEL, and JENNI MOROZUMI. "Concentrated Americans" (audiocassette). San Francisco, California: National Asian American Telecommunications Association, 1985.

NOTES

NOTES

NOTES